The Road to Life

The Road to Life

The Road to Life

Readings for Lent and
Easter from
The Divine Office

HarperCollins*Religious*

HarperCollins*Religious*
Part of HarperCollins*Publishers*
77–85 Fulham Palace Road,
Hammersmith, London W6 8JB

First published in Great Britain
in 1976 by Collins Liturgical Publications,
now part of HarperCollins*Religious*
under the title *Readings for Lent*

The Road to Life is taken from *The Divine Office*,
© 1974 the hierarchies of England and Wales,
Ireland, Australia. Original version of short
responses, responsaries, and second readings,
© 1974 the hierarchies of Australia,
England and Wales, Ireland

A catalogue record for this book is
available from the British Library

ISBN 978-0-00-742464-1

CONDITIONS OF SALE

This book is sold subject to the condition that it
shall not, by way of trade or otherwise, be lent, re-sold,
hired out or otherwise circulated without the publisher's
prior consent in any form of binding or cover other
than that in which it is published and without a
similar condition including this condition being
imposed on the subsequent purchaser.

All rights reserved. No part of this publication may be
reproduced, stored in a retrieval system, or transmitted,
in any form or by any means, electronic, mechanical,
photocopying, recording or otherwise, without the prior
permission of the publishers.

CONTENTS

ACKNOWLEDGEMENTS

The publishers are grateful for permission to reproduce copyright material:

Jerusalem Bible, published and © 1966, 1967, 1968, by Darton, Longman & Todd Ltd, and Doubleday & Company Inc.: extracts from Isaiah, Ezekiel, Hebrews.

Revised Standard Version, Common Bible, copyrighted © 1973, by the Division of Christian Education, National Council of the Churches of Christ in the USA: extracts from Exodus, Leviticus, Numbers, Matthew, Romans. Special permission has been obtained to use in this publication the 'you-your-yours' forms of the personal pronoun in the address to God.

Psalm texts from The Psalms, A New Translation, © copyright 1963 The Grail (England), published by Collins in Fontana Books.

Extracts from *The Documents of Vatican II*, ed. W. Abbot, © The America Press, 1965, published by Geoffrey Chapman Publishers.

Edward Maltesta, trans, *Homily of Melito of Sardis on the Pasch*, nn. 65-71, from *The Way*, vol 2, no. 2, April 1962.

FOREWORD

I recently came across a lovely image for the Church. It was described simply as the 'lunar' model of the Church, and it was attributed to St Didimus the Blind, the mentor of St Jerome. I think it applies to the individual Christian, too.

Put very simply, the image makes clear that just as the moon does no more than reflect the light of the sun, so too the Church has as its sole purpose to reflect the light of Christ.

In our time, astronauts have stood on the surface of the moon. They showed us that it consists of a rough rock surface, pitted and full of craters. Of itself it has little to commend it. In fact the one thing for which the moon is known and loved is not proper to it at all. That, of course, is the wonderful light that can illuminate our darkest nights and inspire such romantic thoughts.

So too with the Church, and, to a lesser extent, the individual Christian. We are called simply to reflect the light of Christ. We have no light of our own. We have no love of our own. What we have to give is what we receive. Our brightness does not depend on our own efforts, but simply on the goodness of God.

The moon, of course, is at its brightest when its full face is open to the distant sun. That is true of the Church, and the individual Christian, too. When we are turned away from Christ, or turned in on ourselves, then we fail to reflect the light of Christ. When our lives are turned consistently to Christ, when He is the centre of our lives our hearts, our effort, then we are in the right place to shine brightly with the light which comes from God.

Lent, of course, is a special season in the Christian year. It is a time when we look again at the fundamental shape and direction of our lives. It is the season of penance and self-denial, not in order to produce a miserable mood for a month or so, but in order to carve out space for God in our busy daily routines. It is the season for taking stock, and for making sure that our lives really are being lived face to face with Christ.

I welcome this book of readings and meditations. They are part of a long, long Christian tradition and I am sure they will help many people to bring into daily life that moment of quiet reorientation to Christ. Moments such as those are capable of transforming a routine, or even oppressive, day into a gift offered to God in return for His gifts of life and light.

Bishop Vincent Nichols
26 September 1993

ASH WEDNESDAY

℣ Repent, and do penance.
℟ Make yourselves a new heart and a new spirit.

THE FIRST READING   Is 58:1-12
A reading from the prophet Isaiah

The fast which is pleasing to God

Shout for all you are worth,
raise your voice like a trumpet.
Proclaim their faults to my people,
their sins to the House of Jacob.

They seek me day after day,
they long to know my ways,
like a nation that wants to act with integrity
and not ignore the law of its God.

They ask me for laws that are just,
they long for God to draw near:
'Why should we fast if you never see it,
why do penance if you never notice?'

Look, you do business on your fastdays,
you oppress all your workmen;
look, you quarrel and squabble when you fast
and strike the poor man with your fist.

Fasting like yours today
will never make your voice heard on high.
Is that the sort of fast that pleases me,
a truly penitential day for men?

Hanging your head like a reed,
lying down on sackcloth and ashes?
Is that what you call fasting,
a day acceptable to the Lord?

Is not this the sort of fast that pleases me
—it is the Lord who speaks—
to break unjust fetters
and undo the thongs of the yoke,

to let the oppressed go free,
and break every yoke,
to share your bread with the hungry,
and shelter the homeless poor,

to clothe the man you see to be naked
and not turn from your own kin?
Then will your light shine like the dawn
and your wound be quickly healed over.

Your integrity will go before you
and the glory of the Lord behind you.
Cry, and the Lord will answer;
call, and he will say, 'I am here.'

If you do away with the yoke,
the clenched fist, the wicked word,
if you give your bread to the hungry,
and relief to the oppressed,

your light will rise in the darkness,
and your shadows become like noon.
The Lord will always guide you,
giving you relief in desert places.

He will give strength to your bones
and you shall be like a watered garden,
like a spring of water
whose waters never run dry.

You will rebuild the ancient ruins,
build up on the old foundations.
You will be called 'Breach-mender',
'Restorer of ruined houses'.

RESPONSORY   Is 58:6,7,9; Mt 25:31,34,35

℟ This is the fast that pleases me, says the Lord: share your
bread with the hungry, and shelter the homeless poor.

* Then you will cry and the Lord will hear; you will call,
and he will say, I am here.

℣ When the Son of Man comes, he will say to the people
on his right, Come, for I was hungry and you fed me.

* Then you will cry and the Lord will hear . . .

THE SECOND READING   Chs 7,4-8,3;8,5-9,1;13,1-4;19,2
A reading from the letter of Pope St Clement I
to the Corinthians

Repent

Let us fix our thoughts on the blood of Christ; and reflect
how precious that blood is in God's eyes, inasmuch as its
outpouring for our salvation has opened the grace of repentance to all mankind. For we have only to survey the generations
of the past to see that in every one of them the Lord has
offered the chance of repentance to any who were willing to
turn to him. When Noah preached repentance, those who gave
heed to him were saved. When, after Jonah had proclaimed
destruction to the people of Nineveh, they repented of their
sins and made atonement to God with prayers and supplica-
tions, they obtained their salvation, notwithstanding that they
were strangers and aliens to him.

All those who were ministers of the grace of God have
spoken, through the Holy Spirit, of repentance. The very
Lord of all himself has spoken of it, and even with an oath:
By my life, the Lord declares, it is not the sinner's death that

I desire, so much as his repentance; and he adds this gracious pronouncement, Repent, O house of Israel, and turn from your wickedness. Say to the children of my people, Though your sins may stretch from earth to heaven, and though they may be redder than scarlet and blacker than sackcloth, yet if you turn wholeheartedly to me and say 'Father', I will listen to you as I would to a people that was holy.

Thus, by his own almighty will, he has confirmed his desire that repentance should be open to every one of his beloved.

Let us bow, then, to that sovereign and glorious will. Let us entreat his mercy and goodness, casting ourselves upon his compassion and wasting no more energy in quarrels and a rivalry which only ends in death.

My brothers, do let us have a little humility; let us forget our self-assertion and braggadocio and stupid quarrelling, and do what the Bible tells us instead. The Holy Spirit says, The wise man is not to brag of his wisdom, nor the strong man of his strength, nor the rich man of his wealth; if a man must boast, he should boast of the Lord, seeking him out and acting with justice and uprightness. More particularly, let us remember what the Lord Jesus Christ said in one of his lessons on mildness and forbearance. Be merciful, he told us, that you may obtain mercy; forgive, that you may be forgiven. What you do yourself, will be done to you; what you give, will be given to you; as you judge, so you will be judged; as you show kindness, so it will be shown to you. Your portion will be weighed out for you in your own scales. May this precept, and these commands, strengthen our resolve to live in obedience to his sacred words, and in humility of mind; for the holy word says, Whom shall I look upon, but him that is gentle and peaceable, and trembles at my sayings?

Thus there exists a vast heritage of glorious achievements for us to share in. Let us then make haste and get back to the state of tranquillity which was set before us in the beginning as the mark for us to aim at. Let us turn our eyes to the Father and Creator of the universe, and when we consider how precious and peerless are his gifts of peace, let us embrace them eagerly for ourselves.

RESPONSORY   Is 55:7;Joel 2:13;cf Ez 33:11
℞ Let the wicked man abandon his way, the evil man his thoughts. Let him turn back to the Lord; he will take pity on him,* for the Lord our God is all tenderness and compassion and ready to relent.
℣ The Lord takes no pleasure in the death of the sinner, but desires he turn from his way and live,* for the Lord our God . . .

THURSDAY AFTER ASH WEDNESDAY

℣ Happy is the man who ponders the law of the Lord.
℞ He will bring forth fruit in due season.

THE FIRST READING   Ex 1:1-22
A reading from the book of Exodus

The oppression of Israel in Egypt

These are the names of the sons of Israel who came to Egypt with Jacob, each with his household: Reuben, Simeon, Levi, and Judah, Issachar, Zebulun, and Benjamin, Dan and Naphtali, Gad and Asher. All the offspring of Jacob were seventy persons; Joseph was already in Egypt. Then Joseph died, and all his brothers, and all that generation. But the descendants of Israel were fruitful and increased greatly; they multiplied and grew exceedingly strong; so that the land was filled with them.

Now there arose a new king over Egypt, who did not know

Joseph. And he said to his people, 'Behold, the people of Israel are too many and too mighty for us. Come, let us deal shrewdly with them, lest they multiply, and, if war befall us, they join our enemies and fight against us and escape from the land.' Therefore they set taskmasters over them to afflict them with heavy burdens; and they built for Pharaoh store-cities, Pithom and Raamses. But the more they were oppressed, the more they multiplied and the more they spread abroad. And the Egyptians were in dread of the people of Israel. So they made the people of Israel serve with rigour, and made their lives bitter with hard service, in mortar and brick, and in all kinds of work in the field; in all their work they made them serve with rigour.

Then the king of Egypt said to the Hebrew midwives, one of whom was named Shiphrah and the other Puah, 'When you serve as midwife to the Hebrew women, and see them upon the birthstool, if it is a son, you shall kill him; but if it is a daughter, she shall live.' But the midwives feared God, and did not do as the king of Egypt commanded them, but let the male children live. So the king of Egypt called the midwives, and said to them, 'Why have you done this, and let the male children live?' The midwives said to Pharaoh, 'Because the Hebrew women are not like the Egyptian women; for they are vigorous and are delivered before the midwife comes to them.' So God dealt well with the midwives; and the people multiplied and grew very strong. And because the midwives feared God he gave them families. Then Pharaoh commanded all his people, 'Every son that is born to the Hebrews you shall cast into the Nile, but you shall let every daughter live.'

RESPONSORY   Gen 15:13-14;Is 49:26
℟ God said to Abraham, Know this for certain, that your descendants will be exiles in a land not their own, where they will be subjected to slavery and oppression for four hundred years,* and I will pass judgment on the nation that enslaves them.

℣ I, the Lord, am your Saviour and your Redeemer,* and I will pass judgment . . .

THE SECOND READING   Sermon 6 on Lent, 1-2
    A reading from the sermons of Pope St Leo the Great

Religious purity is achieved by fasting and by works of mercy

Dearly beloved, the earth is always filled with the mercy of the Lord. For every one of us Christians nature is full of instruction that we should worship God. The heavens and the earth, the sea and all within them, proclaim the goodness and the almighty power of their maker. The wonderful beauty of these inferior elements of nature demands that we, intelligent beings, should give thanks to God.

Now, as we come closer to the season which is specially marked by the mysteries of our redemption, the days leading up to the Easter festival, the need for our religious preparation is proclaimed ever more insistently.

The special feature of Easter is that it is the occasion when the whole Church rejoices over the forgiveness of sin. This forgiveness takes place, not only in the case of those who are freshly reborn through baptism, but also in the case of us others who for some time have been counted among God's adopted children.

Certainly it is true that the water of rebirth initially brings about our new life of grace, but for us all it remains necessary to struggle every day against the rust of our earthly nature. Whatever steps forward we make, there is not one of us who is not always bound to do better. All of us must strive hard and so on Easter day no one should remain bound by the vices of his former nature.

And so, dearly beloved, what every Christian should always be doing must now be performed more earnestly and more devoutly. These forty days, instituted by the apostles, should be given over to fasting which means, not simply a reduction in our food, but the elimination of our evil habits.

To these sensible and holy fasts we should link alms-giving which under the one name of mercy covers a multitude of praiseworthy deeds of charity. Thus all the faithful, even although unequal to one another in their worldly possessions, should be equal in the drive of their spiritual lives.

It is our duty to love both God and our fellowmen and, however we may be hindered in other ways, we are always sufficiently free to wish well to others. The angels sang: Glory be to God on high and on earth peace to men who are God's friends. It follows that, if a man shows love to those in any sort of misery, he himself is blessed, he possesses the virtue of charity, and he is at peace.

There are all manner of possible works of mercy and their very variety implies this for true Christians that both the rich and the poor have opportunities for doing good. Thus, even if we are not all equal in our worldly goods, we can achieve an equal standard in the love of our fellows.

RESPONSORY

℞ This time of fasting opens the gates of heaven to us; let us give ourselves to penance and prayer,* so that we may rejoice with the Lord on the day of his resurrection.

℣ In all things let us prove that we are servants of God,* so that we may rejoice . . .

FRIDAY AFTER
ASH WEDNESDAY

℣ Return to the Lord, your God;
℟ For he is gracious and merciful.

THE FIRST READING   Ex 2:1-22
A reading from the book of Exodus

The birth and flight of Moses

A man from the house of Levi went and took to wife a daughter
of Levi. The woman conceived and bore a son; and when she
saw that he was a goodly child, she hid him three months. And
when she could hide him no longer she took for him a basket
made of bulrushes, and daubed it with bitumen and pitch;
and she put the child in it and placed it among the reeds at the
river's brink. And his sister stood at a distance, to know what
would be done to him. Now the daughter of Pharaoh came
down to bathe at the river, and her maidens walked beside the
river; she saw the basket among the reeds and sent her maid
to fetch it. When she opened it she saw the child; and lo, the
babe was crying. She took pity on him and said, 'This is one
of the Hebrews' children.' Then his sister said to Pharaoh's
daughter, 'Shall I go and call you a nurse from the Hebrew
women to nurse the child for you?' And Pharaoh's daughter
said to her, 'Go.' So the girl went and called the child's
mother. And Pharaoh's daughter said to her, 'Take this child
away, and nurse him for me, and I will give you your wages.'
So the woman took the child and nursed him. And the child
grew, and she brought him to Pharaoh's daughter, and he
became her son; and she named him Moses, for she said,
'Because I drew him out of the water.'

One day, when Moses had grown up, he went out to his people and looked on their burdens; and he saw an Egyptian beating a Hebrew, one of his people. He looked this way and that, and seeing no one he killed the Egyptian and hid him in the sand. When he went out the next day, behold, two Hebrews were struggling together; and he said to the man that did the wrong, 'Why do you strike your fellow?' He answered, 'Who made you a prince and a judge over us? Do you mean to kill me as you killed the Egyptian?' Then Moses was afraid, and thought, 'Surely the thing is known.' When Pharaoh heard of it, he sought to kill Moses.

But Moses fled from Pharaoh, and stayed in the land of Midian; and he sat down by a well. Now the priest of Midian had seven daughters; and they came and drew water, and filled the troughs to water their father's flock. The shepherds came and drove them away; but Moses stood up and helped them, and watered their flock. When they came to their father Reuel, he said, 'How is it that you have come so soon today?' They said, 'An Egyptian delivered us out of the hand of the shepherds, and even drew water for us and watered the flock.' He said to his daughters, 'And where is he? Why have you left the man? Call him, that he may eat bread.' And Moses was content to dwell with the man, and he gave Moses his daughter Zipporah. She bore a son, and he called his name Gershom; for he said, 'I have been a sojourner in a foreign land.'

RESPONSORY   Heb 11:24-25,26,27
℟ It was by faith that Moses, when he grew to manhood, refused to be known as the son of Pharaoh's daughter and chose to be ill-treated in company with God's people rather than to enjoy for a time the pleasures of sin,* because he had his eyes fixed on God's reward.
℣ He reckoned that to suffer scorn for the Messiah was worth far more than all the treasures of Egypt; it was by faith that he left Egypt,* because he had his eyes fixed on God's reward.

THE SECOND READING   Hom 6 on Prayer
A reading from the homilies of St John Chrysostom

Prayer is the light of the soul

There is nothing more worthwhile than to pray to God and
to converse with him, for prayer unites us with God as his
companions. As our bodily eyes are illuminated by seeing the
light, so in contemplating God our soul is illuminated by him.
Of course the prayer I have in mind is no matter of routine, it
is deliberate and earnest. It is not tied down to a fixed time-
table; rather it is a state which endures by night and day.

Our soul should be directed in God, not merely when we
suddenly think of prayer, but even when we are concerned
with something else. If we are looking after the poor, if we are
busy in some other way, or if we are doing any type of good
work, we should season our actions with the desire and the
remembrance of God. Through this salt of the love of God we
can all become a sweet dish for the Lord. If we are generous in
giving time to prayer, we will experience its benefits throughout our life.

Prayer is the light of the soul, giving us true knowledge of
God. It is a link mediating between God and man. By prayer
the soul is borne up to heaven and in a marvellous way
embraces the Lord. This meeting is like that of an infant
crying on its mother, and seeking the best of milk. The soul
longs for its own needs and what it receives is better than
anything to be seen in the world.

Prayer is a precious way of communicating with God, it
gladdens the soul and gives repose to its affections. You should
not think of prayer as being a matter of words. It is a desire for
God, an indescribable devotion, not of human origin, but the
gift of God's grace. As Saint Paul says: we do not know how
to pray as we ought, but the Spirit himself intercedes for us
with sighs too deep for words.

Anyone who receives from the Lord the gift of this type of

prayer possesses a richness that is not to be taken from him, a heavenly food filling up the soul. Once he has tasted this food, he is set alight by an eternal desire for the Lord, the fiercest of fires lighting up his soul.

To set about this prayer, paint the house of your soul with modesty and lowliness and make it splendid with the light of justice. Adorn it with the beaten gold of good works and, for walls and stones, embellish it assiduously with faith and generosity. Above all, place prayer on top of this house as its roof so that the complete building may be ready for the Lord. Thus he will be received in a splendid royal house and by grace his image will already be settled in your soul.

RESPONSORY   Lam 5:20;Mt 8:25
R̠ Will you still be forgetful of us, through the long years leave us forsaken?* Bring us back to you, Lord, and let us find our home.
V̠ Lord save us or we perish.* Bring us back to you . . .

SATURDAY AFTER
ASH WEDNESDAY

V̠ The man who lives by the truth comes into the light;
R̠ So that his good works may be seen.

THE FIRST READING   Ex 3:1-20
        A reading from the book of Exodus

The call of Moses and the revelation of the holy Name of God

Moses was keeping the flock of his father-in-law, Jethro, the priest of Midian; and he led his flock to the west side of the wilderness, and came to Horeb, the mountain of God. And the angel of the Lord appeared to him in a flame of fire out of the midst of a bush; and he looked, and lo, the bush was burning, yet it was not consumed. And Moses said, 'I will turn aside and see this great sight, why the bush is not burnt.' When the Lord saw that he turned aside to see, God called to him out of the bush, 'Moses, Moses!' And he said, 'Here am I.' Then he said, 'Do not come near; put off your shoes from your feet, for the place on which you are standing is holy ground.' And he said, 'I am the God of your father, the God of Abraham, the God of Isaac, and the God of Jacob.' And Moses hid his face, for he was afraid to look at God.

Then the Lord said, 'I have seen the affliction of my people who are in Egypt, and have heard their cry because of their taskmasters; I know their sufferings, and I have come down to deliver them out of the hand of the Egyptians, and to bring them up out of that land to a good and broad land, a land flowing with milk and honey, to the place of the Canaanites, the Hittites, the Amorites, the Perizzites, the Hivites, and the Jebusites. And now, behold, the cry of the people of Israel has come to me, and I have seen the oppression with which the Egyptians oppress them. Come, I will send you to Pharaoh that you may bring forth my people, the sons of Israel, out of Egypt.' But Moses said to God, 'Who am I that I should go to Pharaoh, and bring the sons of Israel out of Egypt?' He said, 'But I will be with you; and this shall be the sign for you, that I have sent you: when you have brought forth the people out of Egypt, you shall serve God upon this mountain.'

Then Moses said to God, 'If I come to the people of Israel and say to them, "The God of your fathers has sent me to you," and they ask me, "What is his name?" what shall I say to them?' God said to Moses, 'I AM WHO I AM.' And he said, 'Say this to the people of Israel, "I AM has sent me to you".' God also said to Moses, 'Say this to the people of Israel, "The Lord, the God of your fathers, the God of Abraham, the God of Isaac, and the God of Jacob, has sent me to you": this is my name for ever, and thus I am to be remembered throughout all generations. Go and gather the elders of Israel together, and say to them, "The Lord, the God of your fathers, the God of Abraham, of Isaac, and of Jacob, has appeared to me, saying, 'I have observed you and what has been done to you in Egypt; and I promise that I will bring you up out of the affliction of Egypt, to the land of the Canaanites, the Hittites, the Amorites, the Perizzites, the Hivites, and the Jebusites, a land flowing with milk and honey.' " And they will hearken to your voice; and you and the elders of Israel shall go to the king of Egypt and say to him, "The Lord, the God of the Hebrews, has met with us; and now, we pray you, let us go a three days' journey into the wilderness, that we may sacrifice to the Lord our God." I know that the king of Egypt will not let you go unless compelled by a mighty hand. So I will stretch out my hand and smite Egypt with all the wonders which I will do in it; after that he will let you go.'

RESPONSORY   Ex 3:14;Is 43:11
℟ God said to Moses, I AM WHO I AM.* Say this to the people of Israel, I AM has sent me to you.
℣ It is I, I, the Lord; no other can bring deliverance·* Say this to the people of Israel . . .

THE SECOND READING   Bk 4,13,4-14,1
A reading from the treatise of St Irenaeus
Against the Heresies

The friendship of God

Our Lord, the Word of God, first of all gathered servants for God but later on he made them free men, as he said to the disciples: No longer do I call you servants, for the servant does not know what his master is doing; but I have called you friends, for all that I have heard from my Father I have made known to you. If you once set about loving God, his friendship will bring you immortality.

Therefore it was not because God needed man that he first formed Adam; he was simply looking for recipients who might receive his benefits. Not simply before Adam was made, but even before any created being whatever existed, the Word was in the Father and gave glory to him, and the Word himself was glorified by the Father as he himself said: Father, glorify me with the glory which I had with you before the world was made.

When he told us to follow him, it was not that he needed our service but that he wanted to bestow salvation upon us. To follow the Saviour is to share in salvation; and to follow the light is to perceive the light.

Those who are in the light, do not themselves cause the light but rather they are lit up by it. They do not help the light but they are helped and illuminated by it.

Similarly, our service to God does not mean that we provide him with anything for he does not need our submission to him. He gives life beyond death and eternal glory to those who follow and serve him. He does this for his servants because they serve him, for his followers because they follow him, but he receives nothing in return. He is rich in everything, he is perfect, he needs nothing from us.

The reason why God seeks the service of men is that, good and merciful as he is, he wishes to bestow blessings on those who persevere in his service. God stands in no need of anyone else, but man stands completely in need of God.

This is man's glory—to remain steadfast in the service of God. Therefore the Lord said to his disciples: You did not choose me, but I chose you. He implied that they did not give him glory by following him but that, because they did follow the Son of God, the disciples were glorified by him. In another place he says: I wish that, where I am, they also may be so that they may see my glory.

RESPONSORY   Deut 10:12;Mt 22:38

℟ The Lord your God asks this of you, only this:* to fear the Lord your God, to love him and to serve the Lord your God with all your heart and all your soul.

℣ This is the greatest and the first commandment:* to fear the Lord your God . . .

WEEK 1: SUNDAY

℣ Man does not live on bread alone.
℟ But on every word that comes from the mouth of God.

THE FIRST READING   Ex 5:1-6:1
A reading from the book of Exodus

The oppression of the People of God

Moses and Aaron went to Pharaoh and said, 'Thus says the
Lord, the God of Israel, "Let my people go, that they may
hold a feast to me in the wilderness." ' But Pharaoh said,
'Who is the Lord, that I should heed his voice and let Israel
go? I do not know the Lord, and moreover I will not let Israel
go.' Then they said, 'The God of the Hebrews has met with
us; let us go, we pray, a three days' journey into the wilderness,
and sacrifice to the Lord our God, lest he fall upon us with
pestilence or with the sword.' But the king of Egypt said to
them, 'Moses and Aaron, why do you take the people away
from their work? Get to your burdens.' And Pharaoh said,
'Behold, the people of the land are now many and you make
them rest from their burdens!' The same day Pharaoh commanded the taskmasters of the people and their foremen, 'You
shall no longer give the people straw to make bricks, as heretofore; let them go and gather straw for themselves. But the
number of bricks which they made heretofore you shall lay
upon them, you shall by no means lessen it; for they are idle;
therefore they cry, "Let us go and offer sacrifice to our God."
Let heavier work be laid upon the men that they may labour
at it and pay no regard to lying words.'
So the taskmasters and the foremen of the people went out
and said to the people, 'Thus says Pharaoh, "I will not give

you straw. Go yourselves, get your straw wherever you can find it; but your work will not be lessened in the least." ' So the people were scattered abroad throughout all the land of Egypt, to gather stubble for straw. The taskmasters were urgent, saying, 'Complete your work, your daily task, as when there was straw.' And the foremen of the people of Israel, whom Pharaoh's taskmasters had set over them, were beaten, and were asked, 'Why have you not done all your task of making bricks today, as hitherto?'

Then the foremen of the people of Israel came and cried to Pharaoh, 'Why do you deal thus with your servants? No straw is given to your servants, yet they say to us, "Make bricks!" And behold, your servants are beaten; but the fault is in your own people.' But he said, 'You are idle, you are idle; therefore you say, "Let us go and sacrifice to the Lord." Go now, and work; for no straw shall be given you, yet you shall deliver the same number of bricks.' The foremen of the people of Israel saw that they were in evil plight, when they said, 'You shall by no means lessen your daily number of bricks.' They met Moses and Aaron, who were waiting for them, as they came forth from Pharaoh; and they said to them, 'The Lord look upon you and judge, because you have made us offensive in the sight of Pharaoh and his servants, and have put a sword in their hand to kill us.'

Then Moses turned again to the Lord and said, 'O Lord, why have you done evil to this people? Why did you ever send me? For since I came to Pharaoh to speak in your name, he has done evil to this people, and you have not delivered your people at all.' But the Lord said to Moses, 'Now you shall see what I will do to Pharaoh; for with a strong hand he will send them out, yea, with a strong hand he will drive them out of his land.'

RESPONSORY   Ex 5:1,3
℟ Moses stood before Pharaoh and said, Thus says the Lord:

*Let my people go, that they may hold a feast to me in the wilderness.

℣ The Lord God of the Hebrews sent me to you to say: *Let my people go . . .

THE SECOND READING   On Ps 60,2-3
A reading from the discourses of St Augustine on
the Psalms

In the person of Christ we were tempted and we overcame the devil

'Hear my cry, O God, listen to my prayer.' Who is speaking? It seems to be one individual but let us see if this is really the case. 'From the ends of the earth I called to you, when my heart was faint.' This shows that it is not one individual, except in the special sense that it is one because Christ is one and we are all members of his body. What individual man calls out from the ends of the earth? The only one who calls from the ends of the earth is that heritage about which it was said to God the Son: 'Ask of me and I will make the nations your heritage and the ends of the earth your possession.'

It follows that it is this, Christ's possession and heritage and body and one Church, this unity which we are, which cries from the ends of the earth. What is its cry? As I have said above, its cry is: 'Here my cry, O God, listen to my prayer; from the ends of the earth I called to you.' This means that these words express my cry to you and the expression 'from the ends of the earth' means that it comes from every quarter of the world.

But why have I cried in this way? 'When my heart was faint.' He shows that he is present throughout all the nations of the world not in great glory but in a state of deep tribulation.

Our pilgrim life here on earth cannot be without temptation for it is through temptation that we make progress and it is only by being tempted that we come to know ourselves. We

27

cannot win our crown unless we overcome, and we cannot overcome unless we enter the contest and there is no contest unless we have an enemy and the temptations he brings.

And so it comes about that this one who cries from the ends of the earth is faint and weak but is not abandoned. He is not alone because according to his plan in his own body he prefigures us who are members of that body. In that body he has already risen again and ascended into heaven and so we his members can trust that, where our head has gone before, we will surely follow.

When he willed to be tempted by the devil, he figuratively transferred us into himself. We have just read in the gospel that our Lord Jesus Christ was tempted in the desert by the devil and this is exactly what happened. In Christ you were being tempted because Christ had his human flesh from you, just as he won salvation for you from himself. He received death from you, just as he gained life from himself for you. From you he received reproaches and from himself for you he gained glory and honour. In the same way he suffered the temptation for you and he won from himself the victory for you.

If we have been tempted in him, in him we conquer the devil. Do you notice that Christ has been tempted and fail to notice that he overcame the temptation? Recognize your own self, tempted in him and conquering also in him. He might have avoided the devil completely but, had he not been tempted, he would have failed to give you the lesson of conquering when you are tempted.

RESPONSORY   Jer 1:19;39:18
R̥ They will fight against you, but shall not overcome you, *for I am with you to deliver you—it is the Lord who speaks. ℣ You shall not fall a victim to the sword; your life shall be safe, *for I am with you . . .

MONDAY

℣ Repent, and believe in the gospel.
℞ The kingdom of God is at hand.

THE FIRST READING   Ex 6:2-13
A reading from the book of Exodus

Second narrative of the call of Moses

God said to Moses, 'I am the Lord. I appeared to Abraham, to Isaac, and to Jacob, as God Almighty, but by my name the LORD I did not make myself known to them. I also established my covenant with them, to give them the land of Canaan, the land in which they dwelt as sojourners. Moreover I have heard the groaning of the people of Israel whom the Egyptians hold in bondage and I have remembered my covenant. Say therefore to the people of Israel, "I am the Lord, and I will bring you out from under the burdens of the Egyptians, and I will deliver you from their bondage, and I will redeem you with an outstretched arm and with great acts of judgment, and I will take you for my people, and I will be your God; and you shall know that I am the Lord your God, who has brought you out from under the burdens of the Egyptians. And I will bring you into the land which I swore to give to Abraham, to Isaac, and to Jacob; I will give it to you for a possession. I am the Lord." ' Moses spoke thus to the people of Israel; but they did not listen to Moses, because of their broken spirit and their cruel bondage.

And the Lord said to Moses, 'Go in, tell Pharaoh king of Egypt to let the people of Israel go out of his land.' But Moses said to the Lord, 'Behold, the people of Israel have not listened to me; how then shall Pharaoh listen to me, who am a man of uncircumcised lips?' But the Lord spoke to Moses and Aaron, and gave them a charge to the people of Israel and to Pharaoh king of Egypt to bring the people of Israel out of the land of Egypt.

RESPONSORY   Cf 1 Pet 2:9,10;Ex 6:7,6
℟ You are a chosen race, a royal priesthood, a dedicated nation, and a people claimed by God for his own. You are now the people of God, who once were not his people. *I will adopt you as my people, and I will become your God.
℣ I am the Lord. I will release you from your labours in Egypt. I will redeem you with outstretched arm.* I will adopt you . . .

THE SECOND READING   Or 14,23-5
   A reading from the addresses of St Gregory Nazianzen

   Let us show one another the Lord's kindness

Acknowledge whence you have existence, breath, and understanding. Acknowledge whence you have what is most important of all, your knowledge of God, your hope of the kingdom of heaven, your contemplation of glory which in this life is of course through a glass darkly but hereafter will be more perfect and clearer. Acknowledge that you have been made a son of God, a co-heir with Christ. Acknowledge, and now I speak with daring, that you have been made divine. From where and from whom have all these benefits come to you?

   Or, to turn to lesser matters, what you see with your eyes, who gave you the power to gaze on the beauty of the sky, the course of the sun, the circle of the moon, and the multitude of the stars? Who gave you the power to discern the harmony and order that shines out like music in them all?

   From whom do you have the rain, agriculture, your food, crafts, dwelling houses, laws and constitutions, civilized life, friendship and intimacy with your relations? To whom do you owe it that some of the animals are tamed and subject to us, and others are given over for our food? Who made you lord and king over everything on earth? Without naming all the individual items, who gave man all the gifts by which he is superior to other living beings?

Surely the answer to all these questions is quite simply God —and God now asks you before all things and in return for all things, to show kindness. When there are so many benefits which we have either received from him or which we hope to receive from him in future, surely we would be ashamed to refuse him this one point in return, namely kindness and love. Although he is our God and our Lord, he is not ashamed to be called our Father, and will we shut ourselves off from those who are related to us?

Brethren and friends, let us by no means be wicked stewards of God's gift to us. If we are, we will have to listen to Saint Peter saying: Be ashamed, you who hold back what belongs to another, take as an example the justice of God, and no one will be poor.

While others suffer poverty, let us not labour to hoard and pile up money, for if we do, holy Amos will threaten us sharply in these words: Hear this, you who say, When will the new moon be over, that we may sell; and the sabbath, that we may open up our treasures?

Let us imitate the first and most important law of God who sends his rain on the just and on sinners and makes the sun shine on all men equally. God opens up the earth, the springs, the streams and the woods to all who live in the world. He gives the air to the birds, the water to the fish, and the basic needs of life abundantly to all, without restriction or limitation or preference. These basic goods are common to all, provided by God generously and with nothing lacking. He has done this so that creatures of the same nature may receive equal gifts and that he may show us how rich is his kindness.

RESPONSORY   Lk 6:35;Mt 5:45;Lk 6:36

℟ Love your enemies and do good, and lend without any
thought of return, and you will be sons of the Most High,*
who causes his sun to rise on bad men as well as good, and rain
to fall on honest and dishonest men alike.

℣ Be compassionate as your Father is compassionate,* who
causes his sun to rise . . .

TUESDAY

℣ Behold, now is the favourable time.
℟ This is the day of salvation.

THE FIRST READING   Ex 6:29-7:25
A reading from the book of Exodus

The first plague inflicted on Egypt

The Lord said to Moses, 'I am the Lord; tell Pharaoh king of
Egypt all that I say to you.' But Moses said to the Lord,
'Behold, I am of uncircumcised lips; how then shall Pharaoh
listen to me?' And the Lord said to Moses, 'See, I make you as
God to Pharaoh; and Aaron your brother shall be your prophet.
You shall speak all that I command you; and Aaron your
brother shall tell Pharaoh to let the people of Israel go out of
his land. But I will harden Pharaoh's heart, and though I
multiply my signs and wonders in the land of Egypt, Pharaoh
will not listen to you; then I will lay my hand upon Egypt and
bring forth my hosts, my people the sons of Israel, out of the
land of Egypt by great acts of judgment. And the Egyptians
shall know that I am the Lord, when I stretch forth my hand
upon Egypt and bring out the people of Israel from among
them.' And Moses and Aaron did so; they did as the Lord

commanded them. Now Moses was eighty years old, and Aaron eighty-three years old, when they spoke to Pharaoh.

And the Lord said to Moses and Aaron, 'When Pharaoh says to you, "Prove yourselves by working a miracle," then you shall say to Aaron, "Take your rod and cast it down before Pharaoh, that it may become a serpent." ' So Moses and Aaron went to Pharaoh and did as the Lord commanded; Aaron cast down his rod before Pharaoh and his servants, and it became a serpent. Then Pharaoh summoned the wise men and the sorcerers; and they also, the magicians of Egypt, did the same by their secret arts. For every man cast down his rod, and they became serpents. But Aaron's rod swallowed up their rods. Still Pharaoh's heart was hardened, and he would not listen to them; as the Lord had said.

Then the Lord said to Moses, 'Pharaoh's heart is hardened, he refuses to let the people go. Go to Pharaoh in the morning, as he is going out to the water; wait for him by the river's brink, and take in your hand the rod which was turned into a serpent. And you shall say to him, "The Lord, the God of the Hebrews, sent me to you, saying, 'Let my people go, that they may serve me in the wilderness; and behold, you have not yet obeyed.' Thus says the Lord, 'By this you shall know that I am the Lord: behold, I will strike the water that is in the Nile with the rod that is in my hands, and it shall be turned to blood, and the fish in the Nile shall die, and the Nile shall become foul, and the Egyptians will loathe to drink water from the Nile." ' And the Lord said to Moses, 'Say to Aaron, "Take your rod and stretch out your hand over the waters of Egypt, over their rivers, their canals, and their ponds, and all their pools of water, that they may become blood; and there shall be blood throughout all the land of Egypt, both in vessels of wood and in vessels of stone." '

Moses and Aaron did as the Lord commanded; in the sight of Pharaoh and in the sight of his servants, he lifted up the rod and struck the water that was in the Nile, and all the water that was in the Nile turned to blood. And the fish in the Nile died; and the Nile became foul, so that the Egyptians could not drink water from the Nile; and there was blood throughout all the land of Egypt. But the magicians of Egypt did the same by their secret arts; so Pharaoh's heart remained hardened, and he would not listen to them; as the Lord had said. Pharaoh turned and went into his house, and he did not lay even this to heart. And all the Egyptians dug round about the Nile for water to drink, for they could not drink the water of the Nile.

Seven days passed after the Lord had struck the Nile.

RESPONSORY   Rev 16:4-5,6,7
℟ The angel emptied his bowl into the rivers, and they turned into blood, and I heard him say, You are the Holy, the Just One, and this is a just punishment,* for they have spilt the blood of the saints and the prophets.
℣ And I heard the altar itself say, Truly, Lord God Almighty, the punishments you give are true and just,* for they have spilt . . .

THE SECOND READING   Chs 1-3
A reading from the treatise of St Cyprian
On the Lord's Prayer

He who gave us life, also taught us to pray.

Dearly beloved brethren, the commandments in the gospel are simply God's teaching. They are foundations on which our hope is based, buttresses for our faith, nourishment to warm our heart, directions for our earthly journey, defences which will help us to preserve salvation. They instruct us, the teachable minds of us, believers here below on earth, and lead us to the kingdom of heaven.

God wanted his servants, the prophets, to say many things which we were to hear but how much more important is what is said by God the Son, what the Word of God, who once spoke in the prophets, now proclaims by his own voice. God is no longer telling us to prepare the way for him who is still to come; rather he himself comes and opens the way for us and shows it to us. Formerly we wandered, blind and reckless, in the darkness of death but now we are enlightened by the light of grace. Now with the Lord for our leader and guide, we can hold to the path of life.

Amidst his many other saving commands and divine precepts with which he took thought for the salvation of his people, he also gave us a form of prayer and taught and instructed us as to what our prayer should be. He who gave us life, also taught us to pray and he did this with the same kindness he showed in his other gifts. While we pray in the presence of the Father with the prayer his Son taught us, we may be more easily heard.

Christ had already foretold that the hour was coming when true worshippers would worship the Father in spirit and truth. He fulfilled what he had promised so that we have been sanctified by him in spirit and in truth and now we are able to give him, as he taught us, worship that is true and spiritual.

What prayer can be more spiritual than the prayer given us by Christ who sent us the Holy Spirit? What prayer in the presence of the Father can be more truthful than that which was pronounced by the Son who himself is the truth? To pray otherwise than as he taught us is more than a mistake, it is a fault, for he laid down: You reject the commandment of God in order to set up your own tradition.

And so, beloved, let us pray as God our Master himself taught us. Our prayer is friendly and intimate when we petition God with his own prayer, letting the words of Christ rise to the Father's ears. When we pray, may the Father recognize his Son's own words. He who dwells in our breast should also be our voice. We have him as our advocate with the Father to plead for our sins and so, when we ask God's pardon for our sins, let us put forward our advocate's own words. He said: Whatever you ask the Father in my name, he will give it to you. Surely it follows that we shall more easily obtain what we ask if, when we pray in the name of Christ, we use his own words?

RESPONSORY   Jn 16:24;14:13

℞ So far you have asked nothing in my name.* Ask and you will receive, that your joy may be complete.
℣ Anything you ask in my name I will do, so that the Father may be glorified in the son.* Ask and you will receive . . .

WEDNESDAY

℣ Repent, and do penance.
℞ Make yourselves a new heart and a new spirit.

THE FIRST READING   Ex 10:21-11:10
A reading from the book of Exodus

The plague of darkness and the announcement of the coming destruction of the first-born

The Lord said to Moses, 'Stretch out your hand toward heaven that there may be darkness over the land of Egypt, a darkness to be felt.' So Moses stretched out his hand toward heaven, and there was thick darkness in all the land of Egypt three days; they did not see one another, nor did any rise from his place for three days; but all the people of Israel had light where they dwelt. Then Pharaoh called Moses, and said, 'Go, serve the Lord; your children also may go with you; only let your flocks and your herds remain behind.' But Moses said, 'You must also let us have sacrifices and burnt offerings, that we may sacrifice to the Lord our God. Our cattle also must go with us; not a hoof shall be left behind, for we must take of them to serve the Lord our God, and we do not know with what we must serve the Lord until we arrive there.' But the Lord hardened Pharaoh's heart, and he would not let them go. Then Pharaoh said to him, 'Get away from me; take heed to yourself; never see my face again; for in the day you see my face you shall die.' Moses said, 'As you say! I will not see your face again.'

The Lord said to Moses, 'Yet one plague more I will bring upon Pharaoh and upon Egypt; afterwards he will let you go hence; when he lets you go, he will drive you away completely. Speak now in the hearing of the people, that they ask, every man of his neighbour and every woman of her neighbour, jewellery of silver and of gold.' And the Lord gave the people favour in the sight of the Egyptians. Moreover, the man Moses was very great in the land of Egypt, in the sight of Pharaoh's servants and in the sight of the people.

And Moses said, 'Thus says the Lord: About midnight I will go forth in the midst of Egypt; and all the first-born in the land of Egypt shall die, from the first-born of Pharaoh who sits upon his throne, even to the first-born of the maid-servant who is behind the mill; and all the first-born of the cattle. And there shall be a great cry throughout all the land of Egypt, such as there has never been, nor ever shall be again. But against any of the people of Israel, either man or beast, not a dog shall growl; that you may know that the Lord makes a distinction between the Egyptians and Israel. And all these your servants shall come down to me, and bow down to me, saying, "Get you out, and all the people who follow you." And after that I will go out.' And he went out from Pharaoh in hot anger. Then the Lord said to Moses, 'Pharaoh will not listen to you; that my wonders may be multiplied in the land of Egypt.'

Moses and Aaron did all these wonders before Pharaoh; and the Lord hardened Pharaoh's heart, and he did not let the people of Israel go out of his land.

RESPONSORY   Cf Wis 18:4;17:20;18:1
℟ A fitting punishment it was for those who had kept your
own sons in prison, that they should be imprisoned in darkness,* for through your sons that law which is light unfailing
was to be given to the world.
℣ Over the Egyptians alone this heavy curtain of night was
spread; brightest of all the light that shone on your chosen
sons,* for through your sons . . .

THE SECOND READING   Dem 11, 11-12
     A reading from the demonstrations of Aphraates

Circumcision of the heart

The law and the covenant underwent a complete change.
First of all God changed the agreement he had made with
Adam and made a fresh one with Noah. God then made a
further agreement with Abraham and he changed this so as
to make a new one with Moses. The covenant with Moses was
not being observed and now in this last epoch of the world
God made yet another covenant but this one is not going to be
changed. God had laid down a law for Adam that he was not
to eat from the tree of life. In Noah's case, as a visible sign of
their alliance, God gave him a rainbow in the sky. For Abraham, chosen on account of his faith, the covenant took the
form of circumcision which would be a mark and character-
istic for his descendants. In the case of Moses the covenant
was signified by the paschal lamb, slain on behalf of the people.
   These covenants were all different from each other. As is
stated by him who laid them down, the real circumcision is
of the kind described by Jeremiah: Circumcise the foreskin of
your heart. If the agreement made by God with Abraham was
firm, this final covenant too is firm and unchanging. God
cannot lay down any further law, whether dealing with those
who are subject to the Mosaic law or with those who are outside the law.

God gave the law with its observances and commandments to Moses. When the Jews failed to keep it, he abolished this law and its commandments and promised a new covenant, different from the old, although he himself is of course the same God who decreed them both. Here is the new covenant which he promised to give: From the least to the greatest among them, they will all recognize me. Now in this final covenant there is no longer any circumcision of the flesh or any other visible sign of the chosen people.

Beloved, we have it as certain that in the different ages of our human story God has set up laws which, for as long as he chose, held good but then fell into desuetude. As Saint Paul says: in each age the kingdom of God once existed under various forms.

Now, our God is truthful and his ordinances are trustworthy; whatever covenant he has ever made was established and proved true for its own time. Those who are truly circumcised in their hearts, live and are circumcised a second time on the other side of the real Jordan, which is baptism for the forgiveness of sins.

When Jesus the son of Nun passed over the Jordan with his people, he circumcised them a second time with a stone knife. Jesus our Saviour circumcises a second time, with circumcision of the heart, those who believe in him and are washed in baptism. They are circumcised with a sword which is his word, sharper than any two-edged sword.

Jesus the son of Nun led the people over to the promised land. Jesus our Saviour promised the land of life to all who, passing over the true river Jordan, have believed and are circumcised in their hearts.

Blessed are those who are circumcised in their hearts and are born again of water in this second circumcision. They will share in the inheritance of Abraham, who was the faithful leader and father of all peoples, because his faith was reckoned to him as righteousness.

RESPONSORY   Heb 8:8,10;2 Cor 3:3
℟ I will establish a new covenant with the House of Israel. I
will put my law into their minds.* I will write it on their
hearts, not with ink, but with the Spirit of the living God.
℣ I will write my law not on stone tablets but on the pages of
the human heart.* I will write it on their hearts . . .

THURSDAY

℣ Happy is the man who ponders the law of the Lord.
℟ He will bring forth fruit in due season.

THE FIRST READING   Ex 12:1-20
                A reading from the book of Exodus

The Passover celebration

The Lord said to Moses and Aaron in the land of Egypt, 'This
month shall be for you the beginning of months; it shall be the
first month of the year for you. Tell all the congregation of
Israel that on the tenth day of this month they shall take every
man a lamb according to their fathers' houses, a lamb for a
household; and if the household is too small for a lamb, then a
man and his neighbour next to his house shall take according
to the number of persons; according to what each can eat you
shall make your count for the lamb. Your lamb shall be without blemish, a male a year old; you shall take it from the sheep
or from the goats; and you shall keep it until the fourteenth
day of this month, then the whole assembly of the congregation of Israel shall kill their lambs in the evening. Then
they shall take some of the blood, and put it on the two doorposts and the lintel of the houses in which they eat them. They
shall eat the flesh that night, roasted; with unleavened bread

and bitter herbs they shall eat it. Do not eat any of it raw or boiled with water, but roasted, its head with its legs and its inner parts. And you shall let none of it remain until the morning, anything that remains until the morning you shall burn. In this manner you shall eat it: your loins girded, your sandals on your feet, and your staff in your hand; and you shall eat it in haste. It is the Lord's passover. For I will pass through the land of Egypt that night, and I will smite all the first-born in the land of Egypt, both man and beasts; and on all the gods of Egypt I will execute judgments: I am the Lord. The blood shall be a sign for you, upon the houses where you are; and when I see the blood, I will pass over you, and no plague shall fall upon you to destroy you, when I smite the land of Egypt.

'This day shall be for you a memorial day, and you shall keep it as a feast to the Lord; throughout your generations you shall observe it as an ordinance for ever. Seven days you shall eat unleavened bread; on the first day you shall put away leaven out of your houses, for if any one eats what is leavened, from the first day until the seventh day, that person shall be cut off from Israel. On the first day you shall hold a holy assembly, and on the seventh day a holy assembly; no work shall be done on those days; but what every one must eat, that only may be prepared by you. And you shall observe the feast of unleavened bread, for on this very day I brought your hosts out of the land of Egypt: therefore you shall observe this day, throughout your generations, as an ordinance for ever. In the first month, on the fourteenth day of the month at evening, you shall eat unleavened bread, and so until the twenty-first day of the month at evening. For seven days no leaven shall be found in your houses; for if any one eats what is leavened, that person shall be cut off from the congregation of Israel, whether he is a sojourner or a native of the land. You shall eat nothing leavened; in all your dwellings you shall eat unleavened bread.'

RESPONSORY   Rev 5:8.9;cf 1 Pet:18,19
℞ The elders fell down before the Lamb, singing a new song:
*Lord, by your own blood, you have purchased us for God.
℣ We were ransomed not with silver or gold, but with the
precious blood of Christ, like that of a lamb without blemish.
*Lord, by your own blood . . .

THE SECOND READING   Hom 13
    A reading from the homilies of St Asterius of Amasea

Let us be shepherds after the style of our Lord

If you want to live up to the standard set by God, you must
imitate his example in whose likeness you are made. You are
Christians and that very name means that you believe in
charity. You must imitate the charity and love of Christ.
Meditate carefully on the richness of Christ's charity. When he
was to appear to man in human fashion, he sent before him
John, a herald of repentance and author of virtue, and, even
before John, there were all the prophets to teach men that
they should change their ways.

Finally, after a short while, Christ came on earth and cried
out personally, with his own voice: Come to me, all you who
labour and are heavy-burdened, and I will refresh you. Look
at how he received those who listened to his voice. He gave
them a ready pardon for their sins and in a moment he
quickly freed them from those who troubled them: the Word
made them holy, the Spirit sealed them, their old nature was
buried, the new man was born and grew young again through
grace. What was the result? He who had been an enemy,
became a friend; he who had been a stranger, became a son;
he who had been common and profane, became sacred and
holy.

Let us be shepherds after the style of our Lord. If we
meditate on the gospels, we will learn as in a mirror how to be
considerate and kind.

Sketched out in the gospel in parables and hidden sayings, I find a man who is shepherd of a hundred sheep. When one of them left the flock and wandered off the shepherd did not stay with those who stayed grazing in the flock without wandering. On the contrary, he went off to search for the single stray, he followed it through countless valleys and ravines, climbed many difficult mountains, searched with great trouble in lonely places, until he found it. When he had found the lost sheep, far from beating it or driving it to return to the flock, he laid it on his shoulders and gently carried it back and returned it to its fellows. The Good Shepherd rejoiced more over this one that was found, than over all the others.

Let us think over the hidden meaning of this parable. The sheep and the shepherd in the story do not refer simply to an ordinary sheep and to the shepherd of dumb beasts. The whole story has a sacred meaning and it warns us not to think of any man as lost or beyond hope. We must not easily despair of those who are in danger or be slow to help them. If they stray from the path of virtue, we should lead them back and rejoice in their return and make it easy for them to rejoin the community of those who lead good and holy lives.

RESPONSORY   Zech 7:9;Mt 6:14
℟ Administer true justice; *show loyalty and compassion to one another.
℣ If you forgive others the wrongs they have done, your heavenly Father will also forgive you.* Show loyalty and compassion to one another.

FRIDAY

℣ Return to the Lord, your God;
℟ For he is gracious and merciful.

THE FIRST READING   Ex 12:21-36
A reading from the book of Exodus

The plague on the first-born of the Egyptians

Moses called all the elders of Israel, and said to them, 'Select lambs for yourselves according to your families, and kill the passover lamb. Take a bunch of hyssop and dip it in the blood which is in the basin, and touch the lintel and the two doorposts with the blood which is in the basin; none of you shall go out of the door of his house until the morning. For the Lord will pass through to slay the Egyptians; and when he sees the blood on the lintel and on the two doorposts, the Lord will pass over the door, and will not allow the destroyer to enter your houses to slay you. You shall observe this rite as an ordinance for you and for your sons for ever. And when you come to the land which the Lord will give you, as he has promised, you shall keep this service. And when your children say to you, "What do you mean by this service?" you shall say, "It is the sacrifice of the Lord's passover, for he passed over the houses of the people of Israel in Egypt, when he slew the Egyptians but spared our houses." ' And the people bowed their heads and worshipped.

Then the people of Israel went and did so; as the Lord had commanded Moses and Aaron, so they did.

At midnight the Lord smote all the first-born in the land of Egypt, from the first-born of Pharaoh who sat on his throne to the first-born of the captive who was in the dungeon, and all the first-born of the cattle. And Pharaoh rose up in the night, he, and all his servants, and all the Egyptians; and there was a great cry in Egypt, for there was not a house where one was not dead. And he summoned Moses and Aaron by night, and said, 'Rise up, go forth from among my people, both you and the people of Israel; and go, serve the Lord, as you have said. Take your flocks and your herds, as you have said, and be gone; and bless me also!'

And the Egyptians were urgent with the people, to send them out of the land in haste; for they said, 'We are all dead men.' So the people took their dough before it was leavened, their kneading bowls being bound up in their mantles on their shoulders. The people of Israel had also done as Moses told them, for they had asked of the Egyptians jewellery of silver and of gold, and clothing; and the Lord had given the people favour in the sight of the Egyptians, so that they let them have what they asked. Thus they despoiled the Egyptians.

RESPONSORY   Cf Ex 12:7,13;1 Pet 1:18,19

℟ The sons of Israel shall take some of the blood of the lamb and put it on the two doorposts and the lintel of their houses. *This blood shall serve as a sign to you.
℣ You were ransomed with the precious blood of Christ, like that of a lamb without blemish.* This blood shall serve as a sign to you.

THE SECOND READING   Bk 3,5

A reading from the book of St Aelred
The Mirror of Charity

Fraternal charity based on the example of Christ

The highest type of brotherly love is to love our enemies and there is no greater encouragement to do this than the remembrance of the wondrous patience exercised by him who, fairest of the sons of men, offered his gracious face to be spat upon by his enemies. All creation is ruled by a glance from his eyes and yet he allowed them to be blind-folded by wicked men. His body he exposed to scourging and, although his head strikes fear in the principalities and powers, he bowed it to the pain of the crown of thorns. He submitted himself to insults and finally gave us an example by enduring in peace with gentleness, patience and meekness, the cross, the nails, the lance, the vinegar and gall. Then as a sheep he was led to the slaughter and, like a lamb before his shearer, he remained silent and did not open his mouth.

Hearing that wondrous voice, full of gentleness and love, saying, 'Father, forgive them,' who would not immediately embrace his enemies? Father, forgive them; can any greater degree of gentleness and love be added to this prayer? However, he did add something. To pray for them was too little, he wished also to make excuses for them. He said: Father, forgive them for they know not what they do. They are great sinners but with little understanding; and so he said: Father, forgive them. They are crucifying without knowing who it is that they are crucifying, for, if they had known, they would never have crucified the Lord of glory, and so he said: Father, forgive them.

They think of him as a law-breaker, as one who falsely claims to be God, and as a seducer of the people. I have hidden my face from them, says the Lord, and they have not recognized my majesty, and so: Father, forgive them for they know not what they do.

It follows that, if a man would really love himself, he should avoid any corrupt love of the flesh. Not to be overcome by fleshly concupiscence, he should turn all his love to the sweetness of the flesh of our Lord. To love his brethren even more perfectly, he should open his arms to embrace even his enemies. In case this divine fire should grow cold by injuries done to him, a man should gaze constantly in his mind on the tranquil patience of his Lord and Saviour.

RESPONSORY   Cf Is 53:12; Lk 23:34

℞ He surrendered himself to death, letting himself be taken for a sinner.* He bore the faults of many while praying for sinners.

℣ Jesus said, Father, forgive them; they do not know what they are doing.* He bore the faults . . .

SATURDAY

℣ The man who lives by the truth comes into the light;
℞ So that his good works may be seen.

THE FIRST READING   Ex 12:37-49; 13:11-16
A reading from the book of Exodus

The Hebrews set out. The law concerning the Passover and the first-born

The people of Israel journeyed from the Rameses to Succoth, about six hundred thousand men on foot, besides women and children. A mixed multitude also went up with them, and very many cattle, both flocks and herds. And they baked unleavened cakes of the dough which they had brought out of Egypt, for it was not leavened, because they were thrust out of Egypt and could not tarry, neither had they prepared for themselves any provisions.

The time that the people of Israel dwelt in Egypt was four hundred and thirty years. And at the end of four hundred and thirty years, on that very day, all the hosts of the Lord went out from the land of Egypt. It was a night of watching by the Lord, to bring them out of the land of Egypt; so this same night is a night of watching kept to the Lord by all the people of Israel throughout their generations.

And the Lord said to Moses and Aaron, 'This is the ordinance of the passover: no foreigner shall eat of it; but every slave that is bought for money may eat of it after you have circumcised him. No sojourner or hired servant may eat of it. In one house shall it be eaten; you shall not carry forth any of the flesh outside the house; and you shall not break a bone of it. All the congregation of Israel shall keep it. And when a stranger shall sojourn with you and would keep the passover to the Lord, let all his males be circumcised, then he may come near and keep it; he shall be as a native of the land. But no uncircumcised person shall eat of it. There shall be one law for the native and for the stranger who sojourns among you.'

'And when the Lord brings you into the land of the Canaanites, as he swore to you and your fathers, and shall give it to you, you shall set apart to the Lord all that first opens the womb. All the firstlings of your cattle that are males shall be the Lord's. Every firstling of an ass you shall redeem with a lamb, or if you will not redeem it you shall break its neck. Every first-born of man among your sons you shall redeem. And when in time to come your son asks you, "What does this mean?" you shall say to him, "By strength of hand the Lord brought us out of Egypt, from the house of bondage. For when Pharaoh stubbornly refused to let us go, the Lord slew all the first-born in the land of Egypt, both the first-born of man and the first-born of cattle. Therefore I sacrifice to the Lord all the males that first open the womb; but all the first-born of my sons I redeem." It shall be as a mark on your hand or frontlets between your eyes; for by a strong hand the Lord brought us out of Egypt.'

RESPONSORY   Cf Lk 2:22,23,24

℟ The parents of Jesus took him up to Jerusalem to present him to the Lord,* as it stands written in the law of the Lord: Every first-born male must be consecrated to the Lord.
℣ They offered to the Lord on his behalf a pair of turtle doves or two young pigeons,* as it stands written in the law . . .

THE SECOND READING
A reading from the Constitution of the Second
Vatican Council on the Church in the Modern World

The broader aspirations of mankind

The modern world shows itself at one and the same time both
powerful and weak, capable of the noblest deeds or of the
foulest. Before it lies the path to freedom or to slavery, to
progress or decline, to brotherhood or hatred. Moreover, man
is becoming aware that the forces which he has unleashed are
in his own hands, and that he himself must either control them
or be enslaved by them. That is why he is putting questions to
himself.

The dichotomy affecting the modern world is, in fact, a
symptom of the deeper dichotomy that is in man himself.

He is the meeting point of many conflicting forces. In his
condition as a created being he is limited by a thousand short-
comings, yet he feels unlimited in his yearnings and destined
for a higher life. Torn by a welter of attractions he is compelled
to choose between them and to reject some of them. Worse
still, feeble and sinful as he is, he often does the very thing he
hates and does not do what he wants. And so he feels himself
divided and the result is a host of discords in social life.

Many, it is true, fail to see the dramatic nature of this state
of affairs in all its clarity for their vision is blurred on the
practical level by materialism, or they are prevented from
even thinking about it by the wretchedness of their plight.

Others delude themselves that they have found peace in a
world-view now fashionable.

There are still others whose hopes are set on a genuine and
total emancipation of mankind through human effort alone and
look forward to some future paradise where all the desires of
their hearts will be fulfilled.

Nor is it unusual to find people who having lost faith in life
extol the kind of foolhardiness which would empty life of all

significance in itself and invest it with a meaning of their own devising.

Nonetheless, in the face of modern developments there is a growing body of men who are asking the most fundamental of all questions or are glimpsing them with a keener insight: what is man? what is the meaning of suffering, evil, death, which have not been eliminated by all this progress? are these achievements worth the price that has to be paid? what can man contribute to society? what can he expect from it? what happens after this earthly life is ended?

The Church believes that Christ, who died and was raised for the sake of all, can show man the way and strengthen him through the Spirit in order to be worthy of his destiny: nor is there any other name under heaven given to men by which they must be saved. The Church likewise believes that the key, the centre and the purpose of the whole of man's history is to be found in its Lord and Master. She also maintains that in all these upheavals there is a great deal that is unchanging, a great deal that has its ultimate foundation in Christ, who is the same yesterday, and today, and forever.

RESPONSORY   1 Cor 15:55-56,57;Lam 3:25
R̰ Death, where is your victory? Death, where is your sting? The sting of death is sin,* so let us thank God for giving us the victory through our Lord Jesus Christ.
V̰ The Lord is good to those who trust him, to the soul that searches for him.* So let us thank God . . .

WEEK 2: SUNDAY

℣ The voice of the Father was heard from heaven:
℟ This is my Son with whom I am well pleased; listen to his word.

THE FIRST READING   Ex 13:17-14:9
A reading from the book of Exodus

The journey of the Israelites as far as the Red Sea

When Pharaoh let the people go, God did not lead them by way of the land of the Philistines, although that was near; for God said, 'Lest the people repent when they see war, and return to Egypt.' But God led the people round by the way of the wilderness toward the Red Sea. And the people of Israel went up out of the land of Egypt equipped for battle. And Moses took the bones of Joseph with him; for Joseph had solemnly sworn the people of Israel, saying, 'God will visit you; then you must carry my bones with you from here.' And they moved on from Succoth, and encamped at Etham, on the edge of the wilderness. And the Lord went before them by day in a pillar of cloud to lead them along the way, and by night in a pillar of fire to give them light, that they might travel by day and by night; the pillar of cloud by day and the pillar of fire by night did not depart from before the people.

Then the Lord said to Moses, 'Tell the people of Israel to turn back and encamp in front of Pi-hahiroth, between Migdol and the sea, in front of Baal-zephon; you shall encamp over against it, by the sea. For Pharaoh will say of the people of Israel, "They are entangled in the land; the wilderness has shut them in." And I will harden Pharaoh's heart, and he will pursue them and I will get glory over Pharaoh and all his host;

and the Egyptians shall know that I am the Lord.' And they did so.

When the king of Egypt was told that the people had fled, the mind of Pharaoh and his servants was changed towards the people, and they said, 'What is this we have done, that we have let Israel go from serving us?' So he made ready his chariot and took his army with him, and took six hundred picked chariots and all the other chariots of Egypt with officers over all of them. And the Lord hardened the heart of Pharaoh king of Egypt and he pursued the people of Israel as they went forth defiantly. The Egyptians pursued them, all Pharaoh's horses and chariots and his horsemen and his army, and overtook them encamped at the sea, by Pi-hahiroth, in front of Baal-zephon.

RESPONSORY   Ps 113:1,2;Ex 13:21
℟ When Israel came forth from Egypt, Jacob's sons from an alien people,* Judah became the Lord's temple, Israel became his kingdom.
℣ The Lord went before them in a pillar of cloud to lead them along the way.* Judah became the Lord's temple . . .

THE SECOND READING   Sermon 51,3-4.8
    A reading from the sermons of Pope St Leo the Great

The law was given through Moses, grace and truth came through Jesus Christ

The Lord revealed his glory in the presence of chosen witnesses, and made that form of his body which he shared with other men to shine with such splendour that his face was as bright as the sun, and his clothes became as white as snow.

By changing his appearance in this way he chiefly wished to prevent his disciples from feeling scandalized in their hearts by the cross. He did not want the disgrace of the passion, which he freely accepted, to break their faith. This is why he revealed to them the excellence of his hidden dignity.

With the same foresight the foundation of his holy Church's hope was laid, so that the whole Body of Christ should realize the nature of the change which it must undergo, and that the members might promise themselves a share in that honour which had already shone around in their Head.

That was what the Lord meant when he described his coming in majesty in these words, 'Then the righteous will shine like the sun in the kingdom of their Father.' The blessed apostle Paul bears the same witness when he wrote, 'I consider that the sufferings of this present time are not worth comparing with the glory that is going to be revealed to us,' and again he wrote, 'For you have died, and your life is hid with Christ in God. When Christ who is your life appears, then you also will appear with him in glory.'

By that miracle the Lord had yet another lesson to teach the apostles, to strengthen them, and to bring them to all knowledge.

Moses and Elijah, that is the law and the prophets, were seen talking with the Lord. Because those five men were there, these words were fulfilled, 'On the evidence of two witnesses or of three witnesses shall a charge be sustained.'

What could be more firmly founded or more certain than God's word, revealed in the ringing tones of both Old and New Testaments in harmony? Here the teaching of the evangelists and the documentary evidence of ancient witnesses harmonize.

The one covenant thus reinforces the other. The signs which went before had promised Jesus under the veil of mystery. But now the blaze of the present glory has shed a dazzling light upon him. This is because, as Saint John says, 'The law was given through Moses, but grace and truth came through Jesus Christ.' In Jesus have been fulfilled the promise of the prophetic images and the purposes of the regulations of the law. By his presence he demonstrates the truth of prophecies, and by his grace makes possible the acts God has commanded us.

The preaching of the holy gospel must establish the faith of all. None must be ashamed of the cross of Christ, by which he redeemed the world.

None must fear to suffer for righteousness' sake. None must doubt that God will fulfil his promises. For through toil comes rest; through death comes life. Jesus has taken upon his own shoulders all the weakness of our humility. If we are steadfast in our acknowledgment and love of him, in him we win the victory he won, and receive the reward that he has promised.

To help us do what he asks and endure our trials in patience, we must have always ringing in our ears these words of the Father, 'This is my beloved Son with whom I am well pleased —listen to him.'

RESPONSORY   Heb 12:22,24,25;Ps 94:8

R̞. You have come to Jesus, the mediator who brings a new covenant. Make sure that you never refuse to listen when he speaks.* The people who refused to listen to him on earth could not escape their punishment, then how shall we escape if we turn away from his voice that warns us from heaven?

V̞. O that today you would listen to his voice: harden not your hearts.* The people who refused to listen . . .

MONDAY

V̞. Repent, and believe in the gospel.
R̞. The kingdom of God is at hand.

THE FIRST READING   Ex 14:10-31
A reading from the book of Exodus

The crossing of the Red Sea

When Pharaoh drew near, the people of Israel lifted up their eyes, and behold, the Egyptians were marching after them;

and they were in great fear. And the people of Israel cried out to the Lord; and they said to Moses, 'Is it because there are no graves in Egypt that you have taken us away to die in the wilderness? What have you done to us, in bringing us out of Egypt? Is not this what we said to you in Egypt, "Let us alone and let us serve the Egyptians"? For it would have been better for us to serve the Egyptians than to die in the wilderness.' And Moses said to the people, 'Fear not, stand firm, and see the salvation of the Lord, which he will work for you today; for the Egyptians whom you see today, you shall never see again. The Lord will fight for you, and you have only to be still.' The Lord said to Moses, 'Why do you cry to me? Tell the people of Israel to go forward. Lift up your rod, and stretch out your hand over the sea and divide it, that the people of Israel may go on dry ground through the sea. And I will harden the hearts of the Egyptians so that they shall go in after them, and I will get glory over Pharaoh and all his host, his chariots, and his horsemen. And the Egyptians shall know that I am the Lord, when I have gotten glory over Pharaoh, his chariots, and his horsemen.'

Then the angel of God who went before the host of Israel moved and went behind them; and the pillar of cloud moved from before them and stood behind them, coming between the host of Egypt and the host of Israel. And there was the cloud and the darkness; and the night passed without one coming near the other all night.

Then Moses stretched out his hand over the sea; and the Lord drove the sea back by a strong east wind all night, and made the sea dry land, and the waters were divided. And the people of Israel went into the midst of the sea on dry ground, the waters being a wall to them on their right hand and on their left. The Egyptians pursued, and went in after them into the midst of the sea, all Pharaoh's horses, his chariots, and his horsemen. And in the morning watch the Lord in the pillar of fire and of cloud looked down upon the host of the Egyptians, and discomfited the host of the Egyptians, clogging their chariot wheels so that they drove heavily; and the Egyptians said, 'Let us flee from before Israel; for the Lord fights for them against the Egyptians.'

Then the Lord said to Moses, 'Stretch out your hand over the sea, that the water may come back upon the Egyptians, upon their chariots, and upon their horsemen.' So Moses stretched forth his hand over the sea, and the sea returned to its wonted flow when the morning appeared; and the Egyptians fled into it, and the Lord routed the Egyptians in the midst of the sea. The waters returned and covered the chariots and the horsemen and all the host of Pharaoh that had followed them into the sea; not so much as one of them remained. But the people of Israel walked on dry ground through the sea, the waters being a wall to them on their right hand and on their left.

Thus the Lord saved Israel that day from the hand of the Egyptians; and Israel saw the Egyptians dead upon the sea-shore. And Israel saw the great work which the Lord did against the Egyptians, and the people feared the Lord; and they believed in the Lord and in his servant Moses.

RESPONSORY   Ex 15:1,2,3
℟ I will sing to the Lord, glorious his triumph! Horse and rider he has thrown into the sea!* The Lord is my strength, my song, my salvation.
℣ The Lord is a warrior! The Lord is his name.* The Lord is my strength . . .

THE SECOND READING   Cat 3,24-7
A reading from the instructions of St John Chrysostom
to catechumens

Moses and Christ

The Jews saw miracles. You will see greater and more glorious miracles than those which accompanied the exodus of the

56

Jews from Egypt. You did not see Pharaoh and his troops drowning; but you saw the devil and his armies overwhelmed by flood waters. The Jews passed through the sea, you have passed through death. They were snatched from the grasp of the Egyptians; you from the grip of demons. The Jews cast off a foreign yoke; you the much more galling slavery of sin.

Shall I tell you of another way which has brought you greater honour than ever they had? Though Moses was their fellow slave and kinsman, the Jews could not bear to look upon his glorified face. But you have seen the face of Christ in his glory. These are the triumphant words of Paul, 'And we all with unveiled faces reflect the glory of the Lord.'

At that time the Jews had Christ to follow them; but in a much truer sense Christ now follows us. Then the Lord walked at their side for the grace of Moses; now the Lord walks at your side not only because of the grace of Moses, but also because of your obedience. Once Egypt had been left behind, the desert awaited them; when your journey is over, heaven awaits you. Their guide, their famous leader, was Moses; our guide and famous leader is another Moses, God himself.

What was the mark of the former Moses? Scripture says, 'Now the man Moses was very meek, more than all the men that were on the face of the earth.' We are not wrong to say that the mark of our Moses is the same. In Christ there is present that most meek and lovely Spirit in closest union, that Spirit which is of one substance with him. Then Moses would raise his hands to heaven and call down from there manna, that is the bread of angels. But our Moses now raises his hands to heaven, and brings us food that lasts for ever. Moses struck the rock and released streams of water; our Moses lays his hand upon the table, he strikes the spiritual board and draws forth the fountains of the Spirit. In its centre there is as it were a fountain, so that the flocks come there from far and wide and are refreshed with its saving waters.

Such is the fountain that we have, this the well-spring of life, this the banquet table abounding with good things past numbering, which makes us strong with spiritual gifts. To it we must come with unfeigned heart and a pure conscience, in order to win grace and pardon before it is too late. This grace and pardon is the gift of the only-begotten Son, our Lord and Saviour Jesus Christ. Through him and with him be glory, honour and power to the Father and to the life-giving Spirit, now and always.

RESPONSORY   Heb 11:24-25,26,27

℟ It was by faith that Moses, when he grew to manhood, refused to be known as the son of Pharaoh's daughter and chose to be ill-treated in company with God's people rather than to enjoy for a time the pleasure of sin,* because he had his eyes fixed on God's reward.

℣ He reckoned that to suffer scorn for the Messiah was worth far more than all the treasures of Egypt; it was by faith that he left Egypt,* because he had his eyes fixed on God's reward.

TUESDAY

℣ Behold, now is the favourable time.
℟ This is the day of salvation.

THE FIRST READING   Ex 16:1-18,35
A reading from the book of Exodus

The manna in the wilderness

They set out from Elim, and all the congregation of the people of Israel came to the wilderness of Sin, which is between Elim and Sinai, on the fifteenth day of the second month after they had departed from the land of Egypt. And the whole congregation of the people of Israel murmured against Moses and Aaron in the wilderness, and said to them, 'Would that we had died by the hand of the Lord in the land of Egypt, when we sat by the fleshpots and ate bread to the full; for you have brought us out into this wilderness to kill this whole assembly with hunger.'

Then the Lord said to Moses, 'Behold, I will rain bread from heaven for you; and the people shall go out and gather a day's portion every day, that I may prove them, whether they will walk in my law or not. On the sixth day, when they prepare what they bring in, it will be twice as much as they gather daily.' So Moses and Aaron said to all the people of Israel, 'At evening you shall know that it was the Lord who brought you out of the land of Egypt, and in the morning you shall see the glory of the Lord, because he has heard your murmurings against the Lord. For what are we, that you murmur against us?' And Moses said, 'When the Lord gives you in the evening flesh to eat and in the morning bread to the full, because the Lord has heard your murmurings which you murmur against him—what are we? Your murmurings are not against us but against the Lord.'

And Moses said to Aaron, 'Say to the whole congregation of the people of Israel, "Come near before the Lord, for he has heard your murmuring," ' And as Aaron spoke to the whole congregation of the people of Israel, they looked toward the wilderness, and behold, the glory of the Lord appeared in the cloud. And the Lord said to Moses, 'I have heard the murmurings of the people of Israel; say to them, 'At twilight you shall eat flesh, and in the morning you shall be filled with bread; then you shall know that I am the Lord your God.'' '

In the evening quails came up and covered the camp; and in the morning dew lay round about the camp. And when the dew had gone up, there was on the face of the wilderness a fine, flake-like thing, fine as hoarfrost on the ground. When the people of Israel saw it, they said to one another, 'What is it?' For they did not know what it was. And Moses said to them,

'It is the bread which the Lord has given you to eat. This is what the Lord has commanded: "Gather of it, every man of you, as much as he can eat; you shall take an omer apiece, according to the number of the persons whom each of you has in his tent." ' And the people of Israel did so; they gathered, some more, some less. But when they measured it with an omer, he that gathered much had nothing over, and he that gathered little had no lack; each gathered according to what he could eat.

And the people of Israel ate the manna forty years, till they came to a habitable land; they ate the manna, till they came to the border of the land of Canaan.

RESPONSORY   Cf Wis 16:20;Jn 6:32

℟ You gave your people the food of angels, sending them bread from heaven already prepared,* containing every delight, satisfying every taste.

℣ It was not Moses who gave you bread from heaven, it is my Father who gives you the true bread from heaven,* containing every delight, satisfying every taste.

THE SECOND READING   On Ps 140,4-6
A reading from the discourses of St Augustine
on the Psalms

The suffering of the entire body of Christ

'I call upon you, O Lord, listen to my prayer.' All of us can make this prayer. This is not merely my prayer; the entire Christ prays in this way. But it is made rather in the name of the body. We can say more than this. For when Christ was on earth he prayed in his human flesh. He prayed to the Father in the name of the body. While he prayed, drops of blood streamed down from all over his body. We read in the gospel, 'In great anguish he prayed more earnestly; his sweat was like drops of blood, falling to the ground.' Surely this bleeding of all his body is the death agony of all the martyrs of his Church.

'I call upon you, O Lord, listen to my prayer. Give ear to the voice of my supplication when I call to you.' Did you think the work of crying out was finished when you prayed, 'I call upon you'? You uttered your cry, but do not think you are now secure. If your tribulation is over, your crying ends. If tribulation continues for the Church, the body of Christ, until the end of time, let it not pray only, 'I call upon you, O Lord, listen to my prayer,' but also, 'Give ear to the voice of my supplication when I call to you.'

'Let my prayer be counted as incense before you and the lifting up of my hands as an evening sacrifice.'

Every Christian recognizes that this is usually understood of the Head himself. As the day was sinking down towards evening, the Lord hanging on the cross laid down his life to take it again. He did not lose his life against his will. We, too, were represented there. What hung upon the cross if not that humanity which he had taken from us? How could God the Father ever desert or abandon his only Son, when the Father and Son are certainly one God? Christ nailed our weakness on to the cross where, as the Apostle says, 'Our old self was crucified with him.' So it was with the lips of this self of ours that Christ cried out, 'My God, my God, why have you forsaken me?'

That is the evening sacrifice, the passion of the Lord, the cross of the Lord, the offering of a saving victim, the whole burnt-offering acceptable to God. That evening sacrifice produced, in his resurrection from the dead, a morning offering. When a prayer is sincerely uttered by a faithful heart, it rises as incense rises from a sacred altar. There is no scent more fragrant than that of the Lord. All who believe must possess this perfume.

'Our old self,' the Apostle tells us, 'was crucified with him that the sinful body might be destroyed, and we might no longer be enslaved to sin.'

RESPONSORY   Gal 2:19-20
℟ I have been crucified with Christ;* I live now not with my
own life but with the life of Christ who lives in me.
℣ I live now in faith: faith in the Son of God who loved me
and sacrificed himself for my sake.* I live now . . .

WEDNESDAY

℣ Repent, and do penance.
℟ Make yourselves a new heart and a new spirit.

THE FIRST READING   Ex 17:1-16
A reading from the book of Exodus

Water from the rock. Struggle with Amalek

All the congregation of the people of Israel moved on from
the wilderness of Sin by stages, according to the commandment of the Lord, and camped at Rephidim; but there was no
water for the people to drink. Therefore the people found fault
with Moses, and said, 'Give us water to drink.' And Moses
said to them, 'Why do you find fault with me? Why do you
put the Lord to the proof?' But the people thirsted there for
water, and the people murmured against Moses, and said,
'Why did you bring us up out of Egypt, to kill us and our
children and our cattle with thirst?' So Moses cried to the
Lord, 'What shall I do with this people? They are almost
ready to stone me.' And the Lord said to Moses, 'Pass on
before the people, taking with you some of the elders of Israel;
and take in your hand the rod with which you struck the Nile,
and go. Behold, I will stand before you there on the rock at
Horeb; and you shall strike the rock, and water shall come out
of it, that the people may drink.' And Moses did so, in the

sight of the elders of Israel. And he called the name of the place Massah and Meribah, because of the faultfinding of the children of Israel, and because they put the Lord to the proof by saying, 'Is the Lord among us or not?'

Then came Amalek and fought with Israel at Rephidim. And Moses said to Joshua, 'Choose for us men, and go out, fight with Amalek; tomorrow I will stand on the top of the hill with the rod of God in my hand.' So Joshua did as Moses told him, and fought with Amalek; and Moses, Aaron, and Hur went up to the top of the hill. Whenever Moses held up his hand, Israel prevailed; and whenever he lowered his hand, Amalek prevailed. But Moses' hands grew weary; so they took a stone and put it under him, and he sat upon it, and Aaron and Hur held up his hands, one on one side, and the other on the other side; so his hands were steady until the going down of the sun. And Joshua mowed down Amalek and his people with the edge of the sword.

And the Lord said to Moses, 'Write this as a memorial in a book and recite it in the ears of Joshua, that I will utterly blot out the remembrance of Amalek from under heaven.' And Moses built an altar and called the name of it, The Lord is my banner, saying, 'A hand upon the banner of the Lord! The Lord will have war with Amalek from generation to generation.'

RESPONSORY   Is 12:3,4;cf Jn 4:14
℟ With joy you will draw water from the wells of the Saviour,* and you will say in that day: Give thanks to the Lord, call upon his name.
℣ The water that I shall give you will become in you a spring of water welling up to eternal life,* and you will say in that day . . .

A reading from the treatise of St Irenaeus
Against the Heresies

Through events which foreshadowed the future Israel learned to fear God and to persevere in his service

From the beginning God formed man in view of his gifts. He chose the patriarchs in order to save them. He began to prepare a people, teaching it, obstinate as it was, to follow him. He provided prophets, to make men accustomed to having God's Spirit within them and to having communion with God. God indeed needed no one's company, but he shared his company with those who needed him. For those who pleased him he set down, like an architect, his plan of salvation. In his own person he gave guidance to his people in Egypt, though they did not see him. To those in the desert, who were restless, he have an appropriate law. To those who entered the good land he gave a fitting inheritance. For those who returned to the Father he killed the fatted calf, and put on them the best robe. In these many ways he blended the human race to a harmony of salvation.

For this reason John said in the Apocalypse, 'His voice was like the sound of many waters.' The Spirit of God is indeed like many waters, because the Father is both rich and great. And the Word, passing through all those men without grudging gave help to all who were obedient by drawing up in writing a law adapted and applicable to every class among them.

By this law he prescribed how they were to make the tabernacle, build the temple, choose Levites, offer sacrifices and oblations, carry out rites of purification, and fulfil all the rest of their service.

He himself has no need of these things. Even before the time of Moses, every good was to be found in him, and the origin of every fragrance, and all the smoke of pleasant incense.

The people were quick to turn back to idols, but God instructed them. Many times he freed them, urging them to persevere in his service. He called them to things of supreme importance by means of things of less importance, that is, he called them by shadows to those things which are real; he called them by temporal things to eternal things, by the carnal to the spiritual, by the earthly to the heavenly. God told Moses, 'See that you make them all after the pattern which you have seen on the mountain.'

For forty days Moses was learning to remember God's words, the heavenly patterns, the spiritual images, the foreshadowing of things to come. Paul, too, says this, 'For they drank from that spiritual rock which followed them; and the rock was Christ.' Paul, again, listed the things which were in the law, and concluded, 'All these things happened to them but they were written down as a warning to us upon whom the end of the ages has come.'

By means of shadows they began to learn the fear of God and perseverance in his service. So the law was both instruction for them and the foretelling of things to come.

RESPONSORY   Gal 3:24-25,23

℟ The Law was our tutor, bringing us to Christ, to find in faith our justification;* when faith comes, then we are no longer under the rule of a tutor.

℣ Until faith came, we were all being kept in bondage to the Law, waiting for the faith that was one day to be revealed.* When faith comes . . .

THURSDAY

℣ Happy is the man who ponders the law of the Lord.
℟ He will bring forth fruit in due season.

THE FIRST READING   Ex 18:13-27
A reading from the book of Exodus

The Judges are given office under Moses

Moses sat to judge the people, and the people stood about
Moses from morning till evening. When Moses' father-in-law
saw all that he was doing for the people, he said, 'What is this
that you are doing for the people? Why do you sit alone, and
all the people stand about you from morning till evening?'
And Moses said to his father-in-law, 'Because the people
come to me to inquire of God; when they have a dispute, they
come to me and I decide between a man and his neighbours,
and I make them know the statutes of God and his decisions.'
Moses' father-in-law said to him, 'What you are doing is not
good. You and the people with you will wear yourselves out,
for the thing is too heavy for you; you are not able to perform
it alone. Listen now to my voice; I will give you counsel, and
God be with you! You shall represent the people before God,
and bring their cases to God; and you shall teach them the
statutes and the decisions, and make them know the way in
which they must walk and what they must do. Moreover
choose able men from all the people, such as fear God, men
who are trustworthy and who hate a bribe; and place such men
over the people as rulers of thousands, of hundreds, of fifties,
and of tens. And let them judge the people at all times; every
great matter they shall bring to you, but any small matter they
shall decide themselves; so it will be easier for you, and they

will bear the burden with you. If you do this, and God so commands you, then you will be able to endure, and all this people also will go to their place in peace.'

So Moses gave heed to the voice of his father-in-law and did all that he had said. Moses chose able men out of all Israel, and made them heads over the people, rulers of thousands, of hundreds, of fifties, and of tens. And they judged the people at all times; hard cases they brought to Moses, but any small matter they decided themselves. Then Moses let his father-in-law depart, and he went his way to his own country.

RESPONSORY   Num 11:25;Ex 18:25

℟ The Lord came down in the cloud and spoke to Moses, and took some of the spirit that was upon him and put it upon the seventy elders;* when the spirit rested upon them they prophesied, and the gift of prophecy never left them.

℣ Moses chose able men out of all Israel and made them heads over the people;* when the spirit rested upon them . . .

THE SECOND READING   On Ps 127,1-3
A reading from the commentary of St Hilary
on the Psalms

Concerning the true fear of the Lord

'Blessed is everyone who fears the Lord, who walks in his ways.' Whenever scripture speaks of the fear of the Lord, we notice that it is never mentioned on its own, as if fear could by itself bring our faith to perfection. Instead, much else is said either before or afterwards to help us to understand the principle of fearing the Lord, and how this fear can be made perfect. This we know from what Solomon says in the book of Proverbs, 'If you would cry out for insight and raise your voice for understanding, if you seek it like silver and search for it as for treasure, then you will understand the fear of the Lord.'

We see how many steps we must climb to come to fear the Lord. First, we must call wisdom to our side. We must hand over to our intellect the whole task of making choices. We must seek wisdom out and track her down. Then we shall understand what it is to fear the Lord. Certainly this is not how the ordinary run of men think about fear.

Fear is the trembling of human weakness frightened of suffering what we do not want to happen to us. This fear is caused in us and stirred by our consciousness of our guilt, or by the power of one stronger than ourselves, or the aggression of one too powerful for us; or it may be caused by sickness, or the attack of a wild animal, or the infliction of any evil.

This fear then is not taught but it comes from our human weakness. We do not learn what we ought to fear. Rather, the things we fear themselves instil their own dread in our minds.

But of the true fear of God we read, 'Come, O sons, listen to me, I will teach you the fear of the Lord.' The fear of God, then, is something to be learnt, because it is taught. Its origins are found by way of teaching, and not in fright. We must find it by obeying commands, by doing the good deeds of a blameless life, and by coming to know the truth, and not in moments of human terror.

All our fear of God is inspired by love; perfect love of God makes fear perfect. We show our love of God especially when we follow his advice, conform to his laws, and trust in his promises. We must follow the words of scripture: 'And now, Israel, what does the Lord your God require of you, but to fear the Lord your God, to walk in all his ways, to love him and to keep his commandments with all your heart and with all your soul, that it may be well with you.'

Many indeed are the ways of the Lord, for he himself is the way. When he spoke of himself, he called himself the way, and he told us why he had done so in these words, 'No one comes to the Father except by me.'

We must, then, examine many ways, and start out on many

of them, so that we may find the one way which is good, the way of eternal life, following the instructions of many different teachers. There are ways provided by the law, or the prophets, or the gospels, or the apostles. We find ways, too, in the various works of the commandments. Those who walk in such ways in the fear of God are blessed.

RESPONSORY   Sir 2:16;Lk 1:50

℞ Those who fear the Lord try to do his will;* and all who love him steep themselves in the law.

℣ He shows mercy to those who fear him, from one generation to another;* and all who love him . . .

FRIDAY

℣ Return to the Lord, your God;
℞ For he is gracious and merciful.

THE FIRST READING   Ex 19:1-19;20:18-21
A reading from the book of Exodus

The promise of the covenant and the appearance of God on Mount Sinai

On the third new moon after the people of Israel had gone forth out of the land of Egypt, on that day they came into the wilderness of Sinai. And when they set out from Rephidim and came into the wilderness of Sinai, they encamped in the wilderness; and there Israel encamped before the mountain. And Moses went up to God, and the Lord called to him out of the mountain, saying, 'Thus you shall say to the house of Jacob, and tell the people of Israel: You have seen what I did to the Egyptians, and how I bore you on eagles' wings and brought you to myself. Now therefore, if you will obey my voice and keep my covenant, you shall be my own possession among all peoples; for all the earth is mine, and you shall be to me a kingdom of priests and a holy nation. These are the words which you shall speak to the children of Israel.'

So Moses came and called the elders of the people, and set before them all these words which the Lord had commanded him. And all the people answered together and said, 'All that the Lord has spoken we will do.' And Moses reported the words of the people to the Lord. And the Lord said to Moses, 'Lo, I am coming to you in a thick cloud, that the people may hear when I speak with you, and may also believe you for ever.'

Then Moses told the words of the people to the Lord. And the Lord said to Moses, 'Go to the people and consecrate them today and tomorrow, and let them wash their garments, and be ready by the third day; for on the third day the Lord will come down upon Mount Sinai in the sight of all the people. And you shall set bounds for the people round about, saying, "Take heed that you do not go up into the mountain or touch the border of it; whoever touches the mountain shall be put to death; no hand shall touch him, but he shall be stoned or shot; whether beast or man, he shall not live." When the trumpet sounds a long blast, they shall come up to the mountain.' So Moses went down from the mountain to the people, and consecrated the people; and they washed their garments. And he said to the people, 'Be ready by the third day; do not go near a woman.'

On the morning of the third day there were thunders and lightnings, and a thick cloud upon the mountain, and a very loud trumpet blast, so that all the people who were in the camp trembled. Then Moses brought the people out of the camp to meet God; and they took their stand at the foot of the mountain. And Mount Sinai was wrapped in smoke, because the Lord descended upon it in fire; and the smoke of it went up like the smoke of a kiln, and the whole mountain quaked greatly. And as the sound of the trumpet grew louder and louder, Moses spoke, and God answered him in thunder.

Now when all the people perceived the thunderings and the lightnings and the sound of the trumpet and the mountain smoking, the people were afraid and trembled; and they stood afar off, and said to Moses, 'You speak to us, and we will hear; but let not God speak to us, lest we die.' And Moses said to the people, 'Do not fear; for God has come to prove you, and that the fear of him may be before your eyes, that you may not sin.' And the people stood afar off, while Moses drew near to the thick darkness where God was.

RESPONSORY   Ex 19:5,6;1 Pet 2:9

℟ If you will obey my voice and keep my covenant, you shall be my own possession among all peoples,* and you shall be to me a kingdom of priests and a holy nation.

℣ You are a chosen race, a royal priesthood, a consecrated nation, a people set apart,* and you shall be to me . . .

THE SECOND READING   Bk 4,16,2-5
A reading from the treatise of St Irenaeus
Against the Heresies

The covenant of the Lord

In Deuteronomy Moses says to the people, 'The Lord your God made a covenant with you in Horeb, not with your fathers did the Lord make this covenant but with you.'

Why did the Lord not make the covenant with your fathers? Because 'The law is not laid down for the just.' Your fathers lived just lives because they had the meaning of the decalogue implanted in their hearts and minds—that is, they loved God, who made them, and they did their neighbour no injury. So they did not need to be warned by written prohibitions; for they had the righteousness of the law in their hearts.

When, however, in Egypt this righteousness and this love

towards God were forgotten and became extinct, God was compelled by his deep love towards men to reveal himself by a voice.

With power he led his people out of Egypt, so that man again might become the disciple of God and follow him. So that they might not despise their creator, he punished those who were disobedient.

He fed them with manna so that they might have spiritual food, as Moses says in Deuteronomy, 'He fed you with manna, which your fathers did not know, that he might make you know that man does not live by bread alone; but that man lives by every word that proceeds out of the mouth of the Lord.'

He taught them to love God, and instilled in them that righteousness which is towards their neighbour. In this way they might be neither unjust nor unworthy of God. By the decalogue he instructed men to be friends with himself and in harmony with their neighbour. Man is greatly helped by these things. God, however, stands in need of nothing from man.

These blessings made man glorious, giving him what he lacked: friendship with God. They bestowed nothing on God, for God did not stand in need of man's love.

Man did not have the glory of God. The only way that man could receive this glory was by obeying God. Therefore Moses said, 'Choose life that you and your descendants may live, loving the Lord your God and obeying his voice and cleaving to him; for that means life to you and length of days.'

To prepare man for this life, God himself spoke the words of the decalogue, to all men alike. And so these words remain with us too. By his coming in the flesh God did not abrogate them; he extended and augmented them. As for the precepts which enslaved, however, God imposed these on his people separately through Moses. These precepts were well devised to instruct or punish them, as Moses himself said, 'The Lord commanded me, at that same time, to teach you statutes and ordinances.'

But by the new covenant of liberty God cancelled those provisions which he had given to his people to enslave them and serve the purpose of a sign. At the same time the laws, which are natural and appropriate to free men and are applicable to all without distinction, were amplified and widened. Out of the abundance of his love, without grudging, God adopted men as his sons, and granted that they might know God as Father and love him with all their heart, and follow his Word without turning aside.

RESPONSORY

℟ Moses, the servant of the Lord, fasted for forty days and forty nights,* so that he might be prepared to receive the Law of the Lord.
℣ Moses went up the mountain of Sinai to the Lord, and stayed there for forty days and forty nights,* so that he might be prepared . . .

SATURDAY

℣ The man who lives by the truth comes into the light;
℟ So that his good works may be seen.

THE FIRST READING   Ex 20:1-17
    A reading from the book of Exodus

The Law is given on Mount Sinai

And God spoke all these words, saying,
    'I am the Lord your God, who brought you out of the land of Egypt, out of the house of bondage.

'You shall have no other gods before me.

'You shall not make for yourself a graven image, or any likeness of anything that is in heaven above, or that is in the earth beneath, or that is in the water under the earth; you shall not bow down to them or serve them; for I the Lord your God am a jealous God, visiting the iniquity of the fathers upon the children to the third and the fourth generation of those who hate me, but showing steadfast love to thousands of those who love me and keep my commandments.

'You shall not take the name of the Lord your God in vain; for the Lord will not hold him guiltless who takes his name in vain.

'Remember the sabbath day, to keep it holy. Six days you shall labour, and do all your work; but the seventh day is a sabbath to the Lord your God; in it you shall not do any work, you, or your son, or your daughter, your manservant, or your maidservant, or your cattle, or the sojourner who is within your gates; for in six days the Lord made heaven and earth, the sea, and all that is in them, and rested the seventh day; therefore the Lord blessed the sabbath day and hallowed it.

'Honour your father and your mother, that your days may be long in the land which the Lord your God gives you.

'You shall not kill.

'You shall not commit adultery.

'You shall not steal.

'You shall not bear false witness against your neighbour.

'You shall not covet your neighbour's house; you shall not covet your neighbour's wife, or his manservant, or his maidservant, or his ox, or his ass, or anything that is your neighbour's.'

RESPONSORY   Ps 18:8,9;Rom 13:8,10
℟ The law of the Lord is perfect, it revives the soul. The rule of the Lord is to be trusted, it gives wisdom to the simple. *The command of the Lord is clear, it gives light to the eyes.
℣ He who loves his neighbour has satisfied every claim of the

law; the whole law is summed up in love.* The command of
the Lord . . .

THE SECOND READING   Chs 6,36;7,44;8,45;9,92
A reading from the treatise of St Ambrose
On Flight from the World

Loyalty to God, One and True and Good

Where a man's heart is, there will be his treasure also, for God
is not wont to refuse a good gift to those who ask. So because
God is good and especially good to those who serve him, we
must cling to him, and be with him with all our soul and with
all our heart and with all our strength. This we must do if we
are to be in his light, and see his glory, and enjoy the grace of
heavenly joy. To this happiness we must lift our minds, we
must be in God, and live in him and cling to him, for he is
beyond all human thought and understanding and he dwells
in endless peace and tranquillity. This peace passes all understanding, passes all perception.

This is the good which permeates everything. All of us live
in it, depend on it. It has nothing above itself, but is divine.
No one is good but God alone, because the good is divine and
the divine is good. So the psalmist says, 'When you open
your hand all creatures are filled with goodness.' Through
God's goodness all the truly good things are given to us, and
among them is no mixture of evil.

These are the good things that scripture promises to the
faithful in the words, 'You shall eat the good of the land.' We
are dead with Christ; in our bodies we carry the death of
Christ, so that the life of Christ also may be manifested in us.
We do not live any longer our own life, but the life of Christ,
the life of innocence, chastity, simplicity, and of every virtue.
We have risen with Christ; we must live in Christ; we must
ascend in Christ, so that the serpent can no longer find our
heel on earth to wound.

We must flee from here. You can flee in your mind, even though you are still held back in the body. You can be both here and you can be present with the Lord if in your soul you cling to him, if in all your thoughts you walk after him, if in faith and not in outward appearance merely you follow his ways, if you fly to him; he is our refuge and our strength. It was to God that David said, 'In you, O Lord, do I take refuge; I have not been put to shame.'

Because God is our refuge and God is in heaven and above the heavens, we must flee from here and come to that place where there is peace and rest from our labours, where we may enjoy the great sabbath feast, as Moses said, 'The sabbath of the land shall provide for you.' To rest in the Lord and to gaze upon his loveliness is truly a feast and full of delight and peacefulness.

We must flee like deer running to the fountains of water. The thirst which David felt, let our soul too feel. Who is that fountain? David said, 'For with you is the fountain of life.' My soul must say to the fountain, 'When shall I come and behold your face?' For the fountain is God.

RESPONSORY   Mt 22:37;Deut 10:12
℟ You must love the Lord your God with all your heart, with all your soul, and with all your mind:* this is the greatest and first commandment.
℣ What does the Lord ask of you? Only this: to fear the Lord your God, to love him, and to serve the Lord your God with all your heart and all your soul:* this is the greatest and first commandment.

WEEK 3: SUNDAY

℣ He gave him the bread of life and understanding to eat.
℟ And the water of wisdom to drink.

THE FIRST READING   Ex 22:20-23:9
A reading from the book of Exodus

The law concerning the stranger and the poor: the code of the covenant

Thus says the Lord:
'Whoever sacrifices to any god, save to the Lord only, shall be utterly destroyed.

'You shall not wrong a stranger or oppress him, for you were strangers in the land of Egypt. You shall not afflict any widow or orphan. If you do afflict them, and they cry out to me, I will surely hear their cry; and my wrath will burn, and I will kill you with the sword, and your wives shall become widows and your children fatherless.

'If you lend money to any of my people with you who is poor, you shall not be to him as a creditor, and you shall not exact interest from him. If ever you take your neighbour's garment in pledge, you shall restore it to him before the sun goes down; for that is his only covering, it is his mantle for his body; in what else shall he sleep? And if he cries to me, I will hear, for I am compassionate.

'You shall not revile God, nor curse a ruler of your people.

'You shall not delay to offer from the fulness of your harvest and from the outflow of your presses.

'The first-born of your sons you shall give to me. You shall do likewise with your oxen, and with your sheep; seven days it shall be with its dam; on the eighth day you shall give it to me.

'You shall be men consecrated to me; therefore you shall not eat any flesh that is torn by beasts in the field; you shall cast it to the dogs.

'You shall not utter a false report. You shall not join hands with a wicked man, to be a malicious witness. You shall not follow a multitude to do evil; nor shall you bear witness in a suit, turning aside after a multitude, so as to pervert justice; nor shall you be partial to a poor man in his suit.

'If you meet your enemy's ox or his ass going astray, you shall bring it back to him. If you see the ass of one who hates you lying under its burden, you shall refrain from leaving him with it, you shall help him to lift it up.

'You shall not pervert the justice due to your poor in his suit. Keep far from a false charge, and do not slay the innocent and righteous, for I will not acquit the wicked. And you shall take no bribe, for a bribe blinds the officials, and subverts the cause of those who are in the right.

'You shall not oppress a stranger; you know the heart of a stranger, for you were strangers in the land of Egypt.'

RESPONSORY   Ps 81:3-4;Jas 2:5
℟ Do justice for the weak and the orphan, defend the afflicted and the needy.* Rescue the weak and the poor; set them free from the hand of the wicked.
℣ Has not God chosen those who are poor in the eyes of the world to be rich in faith and to inherit the kingdom?* Rescue the weak and the poor . . .

THE SECOND READING   Tr 15,10-12.16-17
A reading from the homilies of St Augustine
on St John's Gospel

There came a woman of Samaria to draw water

'There came a woman.' She symbolizes the Church which was not yet justified, but was about to be justified; for this is the effect of the conversation. She comes in ignorance, she finds him, and he converses with her. We must see what this woman of Samaria was and why she had come to draw water. The Samaritans did not belong to the Jewish nation, but were foreigners. It is part of the symbolism that this woman, who is a type of the Church, came from a foreign nation, because the Church was to come from the Gentiles and so be of a different race from the Jews.

We must listen to ourselves speaking in her. We must recognize ourselves in her person; and in her person we must thank God for ourselves. She was not the reality, but its symbol; and because she provided a symbol, she became the reality too. For she came to believe in Jesus, who was putting her before us as a symbol. 'She came to draw some water.' Quite simply she had come to draw water, as any other man or woman is accustomed to do.

Jesus said to her, 'Give me a drink.' For his disciples had gone away into the city to buy food. The Samaritan woman said to him, 'How is it that you, a Jew, ask a drink of me, a woman of Samaria?' For Jews have no dealings with Samaritans.

You see that they were foreigners. Indeed the Jews would not use their vessels. As the woman brought her own bucket to draw some water, she was surprised that a Jew was quite uncharacteristically requesting a drink from her. Although Jesus asked for a drink, his real thirst was for this woman's faith.

Finally, we hear who it is who requests a drink. Jesus answered her, 'If you knew the gift of God, and who it is that is saying to you, "Give me a drink", you would have asked him and he would have given you living water.'

He asks her for a drink and promises to give her a drink. He is in need as one who will accept, he abounds as one who will satisfy. 'If you knew,' he said, 'the gift of God.' God's gift is the Holy Spirit. But he still speaks to her in veiled language, and gradually he enters into her heart. Perhaps he is already teaching her. For what appeal could be more delightful or more kindly made? 'If you knew the gift of God, and who it is that is saying to you, "Give me a drink", perhaps it is you who would have asked him and he would have given you living water.'

The water which he was about to give her is surely the water referred to in the words, 'With you is the fountain of life.' It is impossible for those who 'shall be drunk from the abundance of your house' to be thirsty ever again.

Jesus was promising her plentiful nourishment and the abundant fulness of the Holy Spirit. As yet the woman did not understand. How did she answer in her lack of understanding? The woman said to him, 'Sir, give me this water, that I may not thirst nor come here to draw.' Need drove her to this labour, while her frailty recoiled from it. How wonderful if she heard the invitation, 'Come to me, all who labour and are heavy laden, and I will give you rest.'

That was what Jesus' words to her meant—an end to her labour; but she did not yet understand their meaning.

RESPONSORY   Jn 7:37-39;4:13

℟ Jesus cried out, If any man is thirsty, let him come to me! Let the man come and drink who believes in me! From his breast shall flow fountains of living water.* He was speaking of the Spirit which those who believed in him were to receive. ℣ Anyone who drinks the water that I shall give will never be thirsty again.* He was speaking of the Spirit . . .

MONDAY

℣ Repent, and believe in the gospel.
℟ The kingdom of God is at hand.

THE FIRST READING   Ex 24:1-18
A reading from the book of Exodus

The making of the covenant on Mount Sinai

The Lord said to Moses, 'Come up to the Lord, you and
Aaron, Nadab, and Abihu, and seventy of the elders of Israel,
and worship afar off. Moses alone shall come near to the Lord;
but the others shall not come near, and the people shall not
come up with him.'

Moses came and told the people all the words of the Lord
and all the ordinances; and all the people answered with one
voice, and said, 'All the words which the Lord has spoken we
will do.' And Moses wrote all the words of the Lord. And he
rose early in the morning, and built an altar at the foot of the
mountain, and twelve pillars, according to the twelve tribes of
Israel. And he sent young men of the people of Israel, who
offered burnt offerings and sacrificed peace offerings of oxen
to the Lord. And Moses took half of the blood and put it in
basins, and half of the blood he threw against the altar. Then
he took the book of the covenant, and read it in the hearing of
the people; and they said, 'All that the Lord has spoken we
will do, and we will be obedient.' And Moses took the blood
and threw it upon the people, and said, 'Behold the blood of
the covenant which the Lord has made with you in accordance
with all these words.'

Then Moses and Aaron, Nadab, and Abihu, and seventy
of the elders of Israel went up, and they saw the God of Israel;

and there was under his feet as it were a pavement of sapphire stone, like the very heaven for clearness. And he did not lay his hand on the chief men of the people of Israel; they beheld God, and ate and drank.

The Lord said to Moses, 'Come up to me on the mountain, and wait there; and I will give you the tables of stone, with the law and the commandments, which I have written for their instruction.' So Moses rose with his servant Joshua, and Moses went up into the mountain of God. And he said to the elders, 'Tarry here for us, until we come to you again; and, behold, Aaron and Hur are with you; whoever has a cause, let him go to them.'

Then Moses went up on the mountain, and the cloud covered the mountain. The glory of the Lord settled on Mount Sinai, and the cloud covered it six days; and on the seventh day he called to Moses out of the midst of the cloud. Now the appearance of the glory of the Lord was like a devouring fire on the top of the mountain in the sight of the people of Israel. And Moses entered the cloud, and went up on the mountain. And Moses was on the mountain forty days and forty nights.

RESPONSORY   Cf Sir 45:5,6;Acts 7:38
℟ God allowed Moses to hear his voice and led him into the dark cloud;* face to face, he gave him the commandments, a law that brings life and knowledge, to teach Jacob the covenant and Israel his decrees.
℣ When they held the assembly in the wilderness it was only through Moses that our ancestors could communicate with the angel who had spoken to him on Mount Sinai;* face to face, he gave him the commandments . . .

THE SECOND READING   Hom 20,3
A reading from the homilies of St Basil the Great

Let him who boasts, boast of the Lord

Let the wise man not glory in his wisdom, let not the mighty man glory in his might, let not the rich man glory in his riches.

But what constitutes true boasting, and wherein is a man great? 'Let him who glories in this,' it is written, 'that he understands and knows me, that I am the Lord.'

Herein lies the greatness of man, his glory and his majesty, truly to know what is great, to cling to it, and to seek glory from the Lord of glory. For the Apostle says, 'Let him who boasts, boast of the Lord,' in the passage where he writes, 'God made Christ our wisdom, our righteousness and sanctification and redemption; therefore, as it is written, let him who boasts, boast of the Lord.'

A man glories fully and perfectly in God when he does not extol himself on account of his own righteousness, but knows that he is lacking in true righteousness, and that he is really justified by faith alone in Christ.

Paul boasts of the fact that he despises his own righteousness, but seeks that righteousness by faith which comes through Christ, which comes from God, so that he may know him and the power of his resurrection, and may share his sufferings, becoming like him in his death, that if possible he may somehow attain the resurrection from the dead.

Here all loftiness of pride has fallen. Nothing of which you might boast is left you, O man, so let your boast and your hope be founded on him, so that you mortify all that is yours, and seek your future life in Christ. Since we have the first fruits of this, we are already enjoying it, living totally in the grace and free gift of God.

It is God who is at work with you both to will and to work for his good pleasure. What is more, through his Spirit, God reveals his wisdom, which he predestined for our glorification.

God gives us strength and energy in our toils. 'I worked harder than any of them,' says Paul, 'though it was not I, but the grace of God which is with me.'

God has freed us from dangers beyond all human hope. 'We felt,' he says again, 'that we had received the sentence of death, but that was to make us rely not on ourselves, but on God who raises the dead; he delivered us from so deadly a peril and he delivers us now. On him we have set our hope that he will deliver us again.'

RESPONSORY   Wis 15:3;Jn 17:3
℟ To acknowledge you is the perfect virtue,* to know your power is the root of immortality.
℣ Eternal life is this: to know you, the only true God, and Jesus Christ whom you have sent;* to know your power . . .

TUESDAY

℣ Behold, now is the favourable time.
℟ This is the day of salvation.

THE FIRST READING   Ex 32:1-20
A reading from the book of Exodus

Israel's unfaithfulness: the golden calf

When the people saw that Moses delayed to come down from the mountain, the people gathered themselves together to Aaron, and said to him, 'Up, make us gods, who shall go before us; as for this Moses, the man who brought us up out of the land of Egypt, we do not know what has become of him.' And

Aaron said to them, 'Take off the rings of gold which are in the ears of your wives, your sons, and your daughters, and bring them to me.' So all the people took off the rings of gold which were in their ears, and brought them to Aaron. And he received the gold at their hand, and fashioned it with a graving tool, and made a molten calf; and they said, 'These are your gods, O Israel, who brought you up out of the land of Egypt!' When Aaron saw this, he built an altar before it; and Aaron made proclamation and said, 'Tomorrow shall be a feast to the Lord.' And they rose up early on the morrow, and offered burnt offerings and brought peace offerings; and the people sat down to eat and drink, and rose up to play.

And the Lord said to Moses, 'Go down; for your people, whom you brought up out of the land of Egypt, have corrupted themselves; they have turned aside quickly out of the way which I commanded them; they have made for themselves a molten calf, and have worshipped it and sacrificed to it, and said, "These are your gods, O Israel, who brought you up out of the land of Egypt!" ' And the Lord said to Moses, 'I have seen this people, and behold, it is a stiff-necked people; now therefore let me alone, that my wrath may burn hot against them and I may consume them; but of you I will make a great nation.'

But Moses besought the Lord his God, and said, 'O Lord, why does your wrath burn hot against your people, whom you brought forth out of the land of Egypt with great power and with a mighty hand? Why should the Egyptians say, "With evil intent did he bring them forth, to slay them in the mountains, and to consume them from the face of the earth"? Turn from your fierce wrath, and repent of this evil against your people. Remember Abraham, Isaac, and Israel, your servants, to whom you swore by your own self, and said to them, "I will multiply your descendants as the stars of heaven, and all this land that I have promised I will give to your descendants, and they shall inherit it for ever." ' And the Lord repented of the evil which he thought to do to his people.

And Moses turned, and went down from the mountain with the two tables of the testimony in his hands, tables that were written on both sides; on the one side and on the other were they written. And the tables were the work of God, and the writing was the writing of God, graven upon the tables. When Joshua heard the noise of the people as they shouted, he said to Moses, 'There is a noise of war in the camp.' But he said, 'It is not the sound of shouting for victory, or the sound of the cry of defeat, but the sound of singing that I hear.' And as soon as he came near the camp and saw the calf and the dancing, Moses' anger burned hot, and he threw the tables out of his hands and broke them at the foot of the mountain. And he took the calf which they had made, and burnt it with fire, and ground it to powder, and scattered it upon the water, and made the people of Israel drink it.

RESPONSORY   Ps 105:20,21,22;Rom 1:21,23
℟ They exchanged the God who was their glory for the image of a bull that eats grass;* they forgot the God who was their Saviour, who had done such great things in Egypt, such marvels at the Red Sea.
℣ Their empty minds were darkened; they exchanged the glory of the immortal God for a worthless imitation;* they forgot the God . . .

THE SECOND READING   Sermon 43
    A reading from the sermons of St Peter Chrysologus

What prayer knocks for upon the door, fasting successfully begs and mercy receives

There are three things, brethren, three, through which faith stands firm, devotion abides, and virtue endures: prayer, fasting, and mercy. What prayer knocks for upon a door, fasting successfully begs and mercy receives. Prayer, fasting, and mercy: these three are a unit. They give life to one another.

For, fasting is the soul of prayer; and mercy is the life of fasting.

Let no one cut these three apart; they are inseparable. If a man has only one of them, or if he does not have them all simultaneously, he has nothing. Therefore, he who prays should also fast; and he who fasts should also be merciful. He who wants to be heard when he petitions should hear another who petitions him. He who does not close his own ear to a suppliant opens God's ear to himself. The fasting man should realize what fasting is. If anyone wants God to perceive that he is hungry, he should himself take notice of the hungry. If he hopes for mercy, he should show mercy himself. If he desires fatherly kindness, he should display it first. He who wishes someone to make an offering to him should make an offering himself. He is an unworthy petitioner who demands for himself what he refuses to another.

Have this as your norm of showing mercy. Do you yourself show mercy to others in the same manner, amount, and readiness with which you desire it to be shown to yourself.

Therefore, let prayer, mercy, and fasting be one petition for us before God. Let them be one legal aid in our behalf. Let them be a threefold prayer for us.

Therefore, let us seek by fasting what we have lost by our contempt. Let us immolate our souls by fasting, because we can offer nothing better to God. The prophet proves this when he says: 'A sacrifice to God is an afflicted spirit: a contrite and humble heart God does not despise.'

Offer your soul to God; offer the oblation of fasting. Do this to make your soul a pure victim, a holy sacrifice, a living victim, which remains yours while it is given to God. The man who fails to offer this gift to God will have no excuse, for he who will give himself is unable to suffer want.

But, to make those gifts acceptable, follow them up with mercy. Fasting does not germinate unless watered by mercy. When mercy dries up, fasting suffers drought, for mercy is to fasting what rain is to the earth. The man who is fasting may prepare his heart, cleanse his flesh, weed out his vices, and sow virtues. Nevertheless, if he does not sprinkle his plants with streams of mercy, he does not gather his harvest. O you who fast, when your mercy fasts your field fasts, too. O you who fast, what you pour out in mercy comes back as storage in your barn.

Consequently, lest you lose by saving, gather in by dispensing. Give to yourself by giving to the poor man. For you yourself shall not possess what you would not leave to another.

RESPONSORY   Tob 12:8,9
℟ Prayer which is joined to fasting and almsgiving is good,*
for almsgiving will purge away every sin.
℣ Almsgiving is the winning of mercy and of life eternal,* for almsgiving will purge away every sin.

WEDNESDAY

℣ Repent, and do penance.
℟ Make yourselves a new heart and a new spirit.

THE FIRST READING   Ex 33:7-11,18-23;34:5-9,29-35
                        A reading from the book of Exodus

The full revelation of God made to Moses

Moses used to take the tent and pitch it outside the camp, far off from the camp; and he called it the tent of meeting. And every one who sought the Lord would go out to the tent of meeting, which was outside the camp. Whenever Moses went out to the tent, all the people rose up, and every man stood at his tent door, and looked after Moses, until he had gone into the tent. When Moses entered the tent, the pillar of cloud would descend and stand at the door of the tent, and the Lord would speak with Moses. And when all the people saw the pillar of cloud standing at the door of the tent, all the people would rise up and worship, every man at his tent door. Thus the Lord used to speak to Moses face to face, as a man speaks to his friend. When Moses turned again into the camp, his servant Joshua the son of Nun, a young man, did not depart from the tent.

Moses said to the Lord, 'I pray you, show me your glory.' And he said, 'I will make all my goodness pass before you, and will proclaim before you my name "The Lord"; and I will be gracious to whom I will be gracious, and will show mercy on whom I will show mercy. But,' he said, 'you cannot see my face; for man shall not see me and live.' And the Lord said, 'Behold, there is a place by me where you shall stand upon the rock; and while my glory passes by I will put you in a cleft of the rock, and I will cover you with my hand until I have passed by; then I will take away my hand, and you shall see my back; but my face shall not be seen.'

And the Lord descended in the cloud and stood with him there, and proclaimed the name of the Lord. The Lord passed before him, and proclaimed, 'The Lord, the Lord, a God merciful and gracious, slow to anger, and abounding in steadfast love and faithfulness, keeping steadfast love for thousands, forgiving iniquity and transgression and sin, but who will by no means clear the guilty, visiting the iniquity of the fathers upon the children and the children's children, to the third and the fourth generation.' And Moses made haste to bow his head toward the earth, and worshipped. And he said, 'If now I have found favour in your sight, O Lord, let the Lord, I pray you, go in the midst of us, although it is a stiff-necked people; and pardon our iniquity and our sin, and take us for your inheritance.'

When Moses came down from Mount Sinai, with the two tables of the testimony in his hand as he came down from the mountain, Moses did not know that the skin of his face shone because he had been talking with God. And when Aaron and all the people of Israel saw Moses, behold, the skin of his face shone, and they were afraid to come near him. But Moses called to them; and Aaron and all the leaders of the congregation returned to him, and Moses talked with them. And afterward all the people of Israel came near, and he gave them in commandment all that the Lord had spoken with him in Mount Sinai. And when Moses had finished speaking with them, he put a veil on his face; but whenever Moses went in before the Lord to speak with him, he took the veil off, until he came out; and when he came out, and told the people of Israel what he was commanded, the people of Israel saw the face of Moses, that the skin of Moses' face shone; and Moses would put the veil upon his face again, until he went in to speak with him.

RESPONSORY   2 Cor 3:13,18,15

℟ Moses put a veil over his face, so that the people of Israel would not see its brightness;* all of us, however, reflect the glory of the Lord with uncovered faces; and that same glory, coming from the Lord who is the Spirit, transforms us into his very likeness, in an ever greater degree of glory.

℣ To this very day their minds are covered with the same veil;* all of us, however, reflect the glory of the Lord . . .

THE SECOND READING   Bk 1,2.7

A reading from the book of St Theophilus of Antioch
addressed to Autolycus

The vision of God

If you say, 'Show me your God,' I reply, 'Show me the man that you are and I will show you my God.' You must show me that the eyes of your soul can see and that the ears of your heart can hear. Those who see with bodily eyes contemplate the affairs of life on earth and distinguish things that differ, such as light from darkness, white from black, ugly from beautiful, the excessive from the defective, what is well proportioned and shapely from what is irregular and distorted. So too, the human ear distinguishes sounds that are shrill or deep or sweet. In the same way the ears of the heart and the eyes of the soul are capable of perceiving God. For God is seen by those who are capable of seeing him, once they have the eyes of the soul opened. All men have eyes, but some have eyes which are hooded by cataracts and do not see the light of the sun. But the light of the sun does not fail to shine just because the blind do not see; the blind must blame themselves and their eyes. So you also have cataracts over the eyes of your soul because of your sins and wicked deeds.

Just as a man must keep a mirror polished, so he must keep his soul pure. When there is rust on a mirror, a man's face cannot be seen in it; so also when there is sin in a man, such a man cannot see God.

But if you will you can be cured. Deliver yourself to the physician, and he will cure the eyes of your soul and heart. Who is the physician? He is God, who heals and gives life through the Word and wisdom. God made everything through his Word and wisdom, for by his Word the heavens were made firm and by his Spirit all their power. His wisdom is most powerful: God by wisdom founded the earth; he prepared the heavens by intelligence; by knowledge the abysses were broken up and the clouds poured forth dew.

If you know these things, and live in purity, holiness, and righteousness, you can see God. But before all, faith and the fear of God must take the lead in your heart; then you will understand these things. When you put off what is mortal and put on imperishability, then you will rightly see God. For God raises up your flesh immortal with your soul; after becoming immortal you will then see the Immortal, if you believe in him now.

RESPONSORY   Cf 2 Cor 6:2,4,5,7

℟ Now is the time of pardon, this is the day of salvation: let us try to win approval by steadfast endurance and sustained fasting;* we must be armed with the weapons of innocence and rely on the power of God.

℣ In all things let us prove ourselves servants of God by our steadfast endurance and sustained fasting;* we must be armed . . .

THURSDAY

℣ Happy is the man who ponders the law of the Lord.
℟ He will bring forth fruit in due season.

THE FIRST READING   Ex 34:10-28
A reading from the book of Exodus

Second version of the Code of the Covenant

The Lord said to Moses, 'Behold, I make a covenant. Before all your people I will do marvels, such as have not been wrought in all the earth or in any nation; and all the people among whom you are shall see the work of the Lord; for it is a terrible thing that I will do with you.

'Observe what I command you this day. Behold, I will drive out before you the Amorites, the Canaanites, the Hittites, the Perizzites, the Hivites, and the Jebusites. Take heed to yourself, lest you make a covenant with the inhabitants of the land whither you go, lest it become a snare in the midst of you. You shall tear down their altars, and break their pillars, and cut down their Asherim (for you shall worship no other god, for the Lord, whose name is Jealous, is a jealous God), lest you make a covenant with the inhabitants of the land, and when they play the harlot after their gods and sacrifice to their gods and one invites you, you eat of his sacrifice, and you take of their daughters for your sons, and their daughters play the harlot after their gods and make your sons play the harlot after their gods.

'You shall make for yourself no molten gods.

'The feast of unleavened bread you shall keep. Seven days you shall eat unleavened bread, as I commanded you, at the time appointed in the month Abib; for in the month Abib you came out from Egypt. All that opens the womb is mine, all your male cattle, the firstlings of cow and sheep. The firstling of an ass you shall redeem with a lamb, or if you will not redeem it you shall break its neck. All the first-born of your sons you shall redeem. And none shall appear before me empty.

'Six days you shall work, but on the seventh day you shall rest; in ploughing time and in harvest you shall rest. And you shall observe the feast of weeks, the first fruits of wheat harvest, and the feast of ingathering at the year's end. Three times in the year shall all your males appear before the Lord God, the God of Israel. For I will cast out nations before you, and enlarge your borders; neither shall any man desire your land, when you go up to appear before the Lord your God three times in the year.

'You shall not offer the blood of my sacrifice with leaven; neither shall the sacrifice of the feast of the passover be left until the morning. The first of the first fruits of your ground you shall bring to the house of the Lord your God. You shall not boil a kid in its mother's milk.'

And the Lord said to Moses, 'Write these words; in accordance with these words I have made a covenant with you and with Israel.' And he was there with the Lord forty days and forty nights; he neither ate bread nor drank water. And he wrote upon the tables the words of the covenant, the ten commandments.

RESPONSORY   Jn 1:17,18;2 Cor 3:18
℟ Through Moses the Law was given to us; through Jesus
Christ grace and truth have come to us.* No one has ever seen
God; it is the only Son who is nearest to the Father's heart
who has made him known.
℣ It is given to us, all alike, to catch the glory of the Lord as
in a mirror, with faces unveiled; and so we become trans-
figured into the same likeness, borrowing glory from glory.
*No one has ever seen God . . .

THE SECOND READING   Chs 28-9
    A reading from the treatise of Tertullian *On Prayer*

The spiritual offering

Prayer is the spiritual offering which has abolished the ancient
sacrifices. 'What to me is the multitude of your sacrifices?' says
the Lord. 'I have had enough of burnt offerings of rams; I
have no desire for the fat of lambs or the blood of bulls and of
goats. Who looked for these from your hands?' We learn from
the gospel what God has asked for. 'The hour will come,' we
are told, 'when true worshippers will worship the Father in
spirit and truth. God is spirit, and so this is the kind of wor-
shipper he wants.'
    We are the true worshippers and the true priests: praying
in spirit, we make our sacrifice of prayer in spirit, an offering
which is God's own and acceptable to him. This is the offering
which he has asked for, and which he has provided for himself.
This is the sacrifice, offered from the heart, fed on faith, prepared by truth, unblemished in innocence, pure in chastity,
garlanded with love, which we must bring to God's altar, in a
procession of good works, to the accompaniment of psalms
and hymns. It will obtain for us from God all that we ask.
    What will God deny to a prayer which proceeds from spirit
and truth, seeing it is he who demands it? How great are the
proofs of its efficacy which we read and hear and believe. The

old prayer, no doubt, brought deliverance from fire, wild beasts and hunger, and yet it had not received its form from Christ: how much more fully efficacious then is Christian prayer!

It does not station the angel of the dew in the midst of the fire, nor block the mouths of lions, nor transfer to the hungry the peasants' dinner. It has no special grace to avert the experience of suffering, but it arms with endurance those who do suffer, who grieve, who are pained. It makes grace multiply in power, so that faith may know what it obtains from the Lord, while it understands what, for God's name's sake it is suffering.

In the past prayer induced plagues, put to flight the hosts of the enemy, brought on drought. Now, however, the prayer of righteousness turns aside the whole wrath of God, is concerned for enemies, makes supplication for persecutors. Is it surprising that it knows how to squeeze out the waters of heaven, seeing it did have power even to ask for fire and obtain it? Prayer alone it is that conquers God. But it was Christ's wish for it to work no evil: he has conferred upon it all power concerning good.

And so its only knowledge is how to call back the souls of the deceased from the very highway of death, to straighten the feeble, to heal the sick, to cleanse the devil-possessed, to open the bars of the prison, to loose the bands of the innocent. It also absolves sins, drives back temptations, quenches persecutions, strengthens the weak-hearted, delights the high-minded, brings home wayfarers, stills the waves, confounds robbers, feeds the poor, rules the rich, lifts up the fallen, supports the unstable, upholds them that stand.

The angels too pray, all of them. The whole creation prays. Cattle and wild beasts pray, and bend their knees, and in coming forth from their stalls and lairs look up to heaven, their mouth not idle, making the spirit move in their own fashion. Moreover the birds taking flight lift themselves up to heaven and instead of hands spread out the cross of their

95

wings, while saying something which may be supposed to be a prayer. What more then of the obligation of prayer? Even the Lord himself prayed: to him be honour and power for ever and ever.

RESPONSORY   Cf Jn 4:23-24

℟ True worshippers will worship the Father in spirit and truth:* the Father seeks men like these to worship him.
℣ God is spirit, and those who worship him must worship in spirit and truth;* the Father seeks men like these to worship him.

FRIDAY

℣ Return to the Lord, your God;
℟ For he is gracious and merciful.

THE FIRST READING   Ex 35:30-36:1;37:1-9
A reading from the book of Exodus

The making of the sanctuary and the ark

Moses said to the people of Israel, 'See, the Lord has called by name Bezalel the son of Uri, son of Hur, of the tribe of Judah; and he has filled him with the Spirit of God, with ability, with intelligence, with knowledge, and with all craftsmanship, to devise artistic designs, to work in gold and silver and bronze, in cutting stones for setting, and in carving wood, for work in every skilled craft. And he has inspired him to teach, both him and Oholiab the son of Ahisamach of the tribe of Dan. He has filled them with ability to do every sort of work done by a craftsman or by a designer or by an embroiderer in blue and purple and scarlet stuff and fine twined linen, or by a weaver—by any sort of workman or skilled designer. Bezalel and Oholiab and every able man in whcm the Lord has put ability and intelligence to know how to do any work in the construction of the sanctuary shall work in accordance with all that the Lord has commanded.'

Bezalel made the ark of acacia wood; two cubits and a half was its length, a cubit and a half its breadth, and a cubit and a half its height. And he overlaid it with pure gold within and without, and made a moulding of gold around it. And he cast for it four rings of gold for its four corners, two rings on its one side and two rings on its other side. And he made poles of acacia wood, and overlaid them with gold, and put the poles into the rings on the sides of the ark, to carry the ark. And he made a mercy seat of pure gold; two cubits and a half was its length, and a cubit and a half its breadth. And he made two cherubim of hammered gold; on the two ends of the mercy seat he made them, one cherub on the one end, and one cherub on the other end; of one piece with the mercy seat he made the cherubim on its two ends. The cherubim spread out their wings above, overshadowing the mercy seat with their wings, with their faces one to another; towards the mercy seat were the faces of the cherubim.

RESPONSORY   Ps 83:2,4:45:5,6
R̷ How lovely is your dwelling place, Lord God of hosts!
My soul is longing for the courts of the Lord.* My heart and my soul sing out for joy to God, the living God.
V̷ God is within the holy place where the Most High dwells; it cannot be shaken.* My heart and my soul . . .

THE SECOND READING   Bk 13,21-3
A reading from the commentary of Pope St Gregory the Great on the book of Job

The mystery of our being made alive

Blessed Job, a type of Holy Church, sometimes speaks with the voice of her members, sometimes with that of her head.

While he is speaking of the members, he is suddenly raised to speak the words of the head. So he adds: 'I suffered these things, although I was free from iniquity, and my prayer to God was pure.'

Although Christ was free from iniquity, he suffered; he committed no sin, nor was guile found on his lips, yet he underwent the pain of the cross for our redemption. He alone offered pure prayer to God beyond all others, for in the very torment of his passion he prayed for his persecutors, 'Father, forgive them, for they know not what they do.'

What purer kind of prayer can be cited or imagined than that which consists of merciful intercession for those who are the cause of the pain one is suffering? So it came about that our Redeemer's persecutors eventually drank as believers the blood which they had spilled in their rage, and proclaimed that he was the Son of God.

Job's next words speak aptly of this blood: 'O earth, cover not my blood, and let my cry find no place to hide in you.' When man sinned he was told: 'You are earth, and to earth you shall return.'

This earth, however, has not hidden the blood of our Redeemer, in that every sinner, receiving the price of his redemption, confesses and praises it, and makes known its worth to all his neighbours.

The earth has not covered his blood because the Church has now preached the mystery of her redemption in all parts of the world.

We must note the words added, 'Let my cry find no place to hide in you.' The blood of the redemption, which we take, is the cry of our Redeemer. For this reason Paul mentions 'the sprinkled blood that speaks more graciously than the blood of Abel'. Now of Abel's blood it had been said, 'The voice of your brother's blood is crying to me from the earth.'

The blood of Jesus speaks more graciously than that of Abel because Abel's blood sought the death of the brother who killed him, but the blood of the Lord won life for his persecutors.

If the mystery of the Lord's passion is to be effectual in us, we must imitate what we receive and proclaim to others what we venerate.

His cry finds in us a place to hide if the tongue is silent of what the mind has come to believe. But that his cry should not be hidden in us, it remains that each one of us according to his measure should make known the mystery of his being made alive.

RESPONSORY   Cf Gen 4:10,11;Heb 12:24
℟ Lord, hear the blood of your Son, our brother, crying out to you from the ground.* Blessed is the earth that opened its mouth to receive the blood of the Redeemer.
℣ This sprinkling of blood pleads more insistently than the blood of Abel.* Blessed is the earth . . .

SATURDAY

℣ The man who lives by the truth comes into the light.
℟ So that his good works may be seen.

THE FIRST READING   Ex 40:16-38
    A reading from the book of Exodus

The tabernacle is erected. The Glory of God in the cloud

According to all that the Lord commanded him, so Moses did. And in the first month in the second year, on the first day of the month, the tabernacle was erected. Moses erected the tabernacle; he laid its bases, and set up its frames, and put in its poles, and raised up its pillars; and he spread the tent over the tabernacle, and put the covering of the tent over it, as the Lord had commanded Moses. And he took the testimony and put it into the ark, and put the poles on the ark, and set the mercy seat above on the ark; and he brought the ark into the tabernacle, and set up the veil of the screen, and screened the ark of the testimony; as the Lord had commanded Moses. And he put the table in the tent of meeting, on the north side of the tabernacle, outside the veil, and set the bread in order on it before the Lord; as the Lord had commanded Moses. And he put the lampstand in the tent of meeting, opposite the table on the south side of the tabernacle, and set up the lamps before the Lord; as the Lord had commanded Moses. And he put the golden altar in the tent of meeting before the veil, and burnt fragrant incense upon it; as the Lord had commanded Moses. And he put in place the screen for the door of the tabernacle. And he set the altar of burnt offering at the door of the tabernacle of the tent of meeting, and offered upon it the burnt offering and the cereal offering; as the Lord had commanded Moses. And he set the laver between the tent of meeting and the altar, and put water in it for washing, with which Moses and Aaron and his sons washed their hands and their feet; when they went into the tent of meeting, and when they approached the altar, they washed; as the Lord commanded Moses. And he erected the court round the tabernacle and the altar, and set up the screen of the gate of the court. So Moses finished the work.

Then the cloud covered the tent of meeting, and the glory of the Lord filled the tabernacle. And Moses was not able to enter the tent of meeting, because the cloud abode upon it, and the glory of the Lord filled the tabernacle. Throughout all their journeys, whenever the cloud was taken up from over the tabernacle, the people of Israel would go onward; but if the cloud was not taken up, then they did not go onward till the day that it was taken up. For throughout all their journeys the cloud of the Lord was upon the tabernacle by day, and fire was in it by night, in the sight of all the house of Israel.

RESPONSORY   1 Cor 10:1,2;Ex 40:32,33

℟ Our fathers were all guided by a cloud, and all passed through the sea;* in this cloud they were all baptized as followers of Moses.

℣ The glory of the Lord filled the tabernacle because of the cloud that rested on it;* in this cloud . . .

THE SECOND READING   Or 14,38.40

A reading from the addresses of
St Gregory Nazianzen

Let us serve Christ in the poor

Mercy is high in the list of the Beatitudes. 'Blessed are the merciful,' says scripture, 'for they shall obtain mercy.' 'Blessed is he who considers the needy and the poor.' And again, 'it is well with the man who deals generously and lends.' We read elsewhere: 'The righteous man is ever giving liberally and lending.' Let us lay hold of this blessing and earn a name for understanding, let us be kind.

Even the night must not interrupt your works of pity. Do not say, 'Go away and come back. I'll give it to you tomorrow.' Nothing must come between your intention and your carrying out of your act of kindness. Kindness is the only thing which does not admit of delay.

'Share your bread with the hungry, and bring the homeless poor into your house,' and do so with joy and alacrity. 'He who does acts of mercy,' writes the Apostle, 'let him do so with cheerfulness.' Then your good deed is doubled by your readiness. On the other hand, what is offered reluctantly and under constraint is unwelcome and unadorned.

Good deeds must be cheerful, not doleful. 'If you get rid of oppression and unfair preference,' as it is written, that is, meanness and scrutinizing, or ambiguity and grumbling, what will happen? What a great and wonderful thing this is! What a great reward awaits the man who does this! 'Then shall your light break forth like the dawn, and your healing shall spring up speedily.' Now who is there who does not long for light and healing?

If you are willing to listen to me, then, servants of Christ, his brothers and co-heirs, I say that we should visit Christ while there is opportunity, take care of him and feed him. We should clothe Christ and welcome him. We should honour him, not only at our table, like some; not only with ointments, like Mary; not only with a sepulchre, like Joseph of Arimathea; nor with things which have to do with his burial, like Nicodemus, who loved Christ only by half; nor finally with gold, incense and myrrh, like the Magi, who came before all those whom we have mentioned. But, as the Lord of all desires mercy and not sacrifice, and as compassion is better than tens of thousands of fat rams, let us offer him this mercy through the needy and those who are at present cast down on the ground. Let us do this so that, when we depart hence, they may welcome us into the eternal habitations, in the same Christ our Lord, to whom be glory for ever. Amen.

RESPONSORY   Mt 25:35,40;Jn 15:12
℟ When I was hungry, you fed me; when I was thirsty, you gave me drink; when I was a stranger, you took me into your home.* I tell you this: anything you did for one of my brothers here, however humble, you did for me.
℣ This is my commandment: love one another, as I have loved you.* I tell you this . . .

WEEK 4: SUNDAY

℣ Your words, Lord, are spirit and they are life.
℟ You have the words of eternal life.

THE FIRST READING   Lev 8:1-17;9:22-24
A reading from the book of Leviticus

The consecration of the priests

The Lord said to Moses, 'Take Aaron and his sons with him,
and the garments, and the anointing oil, and the bull of the sin
offering, and the two rams, and the basket of unleavened bread;
and assemble all the congregation at the door of the tent of
meeting.' And Moses did as the Lord commanded him; and
the congregation was assembled at the door of the tent of
meeting.

And Moses said to the congregation, 'This is the thing
which the Lord has commanded to be done.' And Moses
brought Aaron and his sons, and washed them with water.
And he put on him the coat, and girded him with the girdle,
and clothed him with the robe, and put the ephod upon him,
and girded him with the skilfully woven band of the ephod,
binding it to him therewith. And he placed the breastpiece on
him, and in the breastpiece he put the Urim and the Thum-
mim. And he set the turban upon his head, and on the turban,
in front, he set the golden plate, the holy crown, as the Lord
commanded Moses.

Then Moses took the anointing oil, and anointed the
tabernacle and all that was in it, and consecrated them. And
he sprinkled some of it on the altar seven times, and anointed
the altar and all its utensils, and the laver and its base, to
consecrate them. And he poured some of the anointing oil on

Aaron's head, and anointed him, to consecrate him. And Moses brought Aaron's sons, and clothed them with coats and, girded them with girdles, and bound caps on them, as the Lord commanded Moses.

Then he brought the bull of the sin offering; and Aaron and his sons laid their hands upon the head of the bull of the sin offering. And Moses killed it, and took the blood, and with his finger put it on the horns of the altar round about, and purified the altar, and poured out the blood at the base of the altar, and consecrated it, to make atonement for it. And he took all the fat that was on the entrails, and the appendage of the liver, and the two kidneys with their fat, and Moses burned them on the altar. But the bull, and its skin, and its flesh, and its dung, he burned with fire outside the camp, as the Lord commanded Moses.

Then Aaron lifted up his hands toward the people and blessed them; and he came down from offering the sin offering and the burnt offering and the peace offerings. And Moses and Aaron went into the tent of meeting; and when they came out they blessed the people, and the glory of the Lord appeared to all the people. And fire came forth from before the Lord and consumed the burnt offering and the fat upon the altar; and when all the people saw it, they shouted, and fell on their faces.

RESPONSORY   Heb 7:23,24;Sir 45:7,8
℟ Of priests there was a succession, since death denied them permanence,* but Christ remains for ever and can never lose his priesthood.
℣ The Lord raised up Aaron to a holy office; he conferred on him the priesthood of the nation and honoured him with glory,* but Christ remains for ever . . .

THE SECOND READING   Tr 34,8-9

A reading from the homilies of St Augustine on
St John's Gospel

Christ is the way to light, to truth, to life

'I am the light of the world; he who follows me will not walk
in darkness, but will have the light of life.' As these few words
of the Lord are partly command and partly promise, let us do
what he commanded, and not merely desire what he promised,
which would be presumptuous; lest he should ask us at the
judgment, 'Have you done what I commanded, that you may
obtain what I promised?' What have you commanded, O Lord
our God? He tells you, 'That you follow me,' You have sought
advice on life. What life, if not that of which it is said, 'With
you is the fountain of life'?

We must therefore get to work, and follow the Lord; we
must break the chains which impede our following him. Now
who can break those shackles unless he is aided by him to
whom it was said, 'You have loosed my bonds'? Another
psalm says of him, 'The Lord sets prisoners free, the Lord
raises up those who have fallen.'

What do those who have been freed and raised up follow if
not the light, of which they have heard, 'I am the light of the
world; he who follows me will not walk in darkness'? For the
Lord gives light to the blind. We are now enlightened, brothers,
helped by the eye-salve of the faith. The Lord's spittle was
once mixed with the earth to anoint the man who was born
blind. We too were born blind from Adam, and need to
be given sight by the Lord. He mixed spittle with earth: the
Word became flesh and dwelt among us. He mixed spittle with
earth; so it was predicted, 'Truth has sprung up from the
earth.' He tells us himself, 'I am the way, the truth and the
life.'

We shall enjoy the truth when we see face to face, for this

too is promised us. Indeed, who would dare to hope for what God had not deigned either to promise or to give?

We shall see face to face. The Apostle tells us, 'Now my knowledge is imperfect. Now I see in a mirror dimly, but then I shall see face to face.' And the apostle John writes in his letter, 'Beloved, we are God's children now; it does not yet appear what we shall be; but we know that when he appears we shall be like him, because we shall see him as he is.' This is a tremendous promise.

If you love, then follow. I do love, you say, but what way am I to follow? If the Lord your God said to you, 'I am the way, the truth and the life,' you, desiring truth and eager for life, would immediately seek the way to attain these. You would say to yourself, 'What a tremendous thing truth is, what a tremendous thing life is, were there only the means by which my soul could reach them.'

Do you ask, by what way? Listen to him saying to you first of all, 'I am the way.' Before telling you whither, he told you by what way. 'I am the way,' he said. The way where? 'And the truth and the life.' First he told you the way to come, then where. I am the way, I am the truth, I am the life. While remaining with the Father, he was truth and life; putting on flesh, he became the way.

You are not told, 'Strive to find the way, that you may come to truth and life.' No, you are not told this. Rise up, you lazy man! The way itself has come to you and awoken you from your sleep, if indeed you have been awakened; get up and walk.

Perhaps you are trying to walk, and are not able because your feet hurt. Why do they? Have they been running over rough ground, spurred on by avarice? The Word of God has cured even the lame. Look, you say, I have sound feet, but I cannot see the way. He has given sight to the blind, too.

RESPONSORY   Cf Ps 118:104-105;Jn 6:68

℞ I hate the ways of falsehood.* Your word is a lamp for my steps, and a light for my path.

℣ Lord, to whom shall we go? You have the message of eternal life.* Your word is a lamp . . .

MONDAY

℣ Repent, and believe in the gospel.
℞ The kingdom of God is at hand.

THE FIRST READING   Lev 16:2-28
A reading from the book of Leviticus

The Day of Expiation

The Lord said to Moses, 'Tell Aaron your brother not to come at all times into the holy place within the veil, before the mercy seat which is upon the ark, lest he die; for I will appear in the cloud upon the mercy seat. But thus shall Aaron come into the holy place: with a young bull for a sin offering and a ram for a burnt offering. He shall put on the holy linen coat, and shall have the linen breeches on his body, be girded with the linen girdle, and wear the linen turban; these are the holy garments. He shall bathe his body in water, and then put them on. And he shall take from the congregation of the people of Israel two male goats for a sin offering, and one ram for a burnt offering.

'And Aaron shall offer the bull as a sin offering for himself, and shall make atonement for himself and for his house. Then he shall take the two goats, and set them before the Lord at the door of the tent of meeting; and Aaron shall cast lots upon the two goats, one lot for the Lord and the other lot for Azazel.

And Aaron shall present the goat on which the lot fell for the Lord, and offer it as a sin offering; but the goat on which the lot fell for Azazel shall be presented alive before the Lord to make atonement over it, that it may be sent away into the wilderness to Azazel.

'Aaron shall present the bull as a sin offering for himself, and shall make atonement for himself and for his house; he shall kill the bull as a sin offering for himself. And he shall take a censer full of coals of fire from the altar before the Lord, and two handfuls of sweet incense beaten small; and he shall bring it within the veil and put the incense on the fire before the Lord, that the cloud of the incense may cover the mercy seat which is upon the testimony, lest he die; and he shall take some of the blood of the bull, and sprinkle it with his finger on the front of the mercy seat, and before the mercy seat he shall sprinkle the blood with his finger seven times.

'Then he shall kill the goat of the sin offering which is for the people, and bring its blood within the veil, and do with its blood as he did with the blood of the bull, sprinkling it upon the mercy seat and before the mercy seat; thus he shall make atonement for the holy place, because of the uncleannesses of the people of Israel, and because of their transgressions, all their sins; and so he shall do for the tent of meeting, which abides with them in the midst of their uncleannesses. There shall be no man in the tent of meeting when he enters to make atonement in the holy place until he comes out and has made atonement for himself and for his house and for all the assembly of Israel. Then he shall go out to the altar which is before the Lord and make atonement for it, and shall take some of the blood of the bull and of the blood of the goat, and put it on the horns of the altar round about. And he shall sprinkle some of the blood upon it with his finger seven times, and cleanse it and hallow it from the uncleannesses of the people of Israel.

'And when he has made an end of atoning for the holy place and the tent of meeting and the altar, he shall present the live goat; and Aaron shall lay both his hands upon the head of the live goat, and confess over him all the iniquities of the people of Israel, and all their transgressions, all their sins; and he shall put them upon the head of the goat, and send him away into the wilderness by the hand of a man who is in readiness. The goat shall bear all their iniquities upon him to a solitary land; and he shall let the goat go in the wilderness.

'Then Aaron shall come into the tent of meeting, and shall put off the linen garments which he put on when he went into the holy place, and shall leave them there; and he shall bathe his body in water in a holy place, and put on his garments, and come forth, and offer his burnt offering and the burnt offering of the people, and make atonement for himself and for the people. And the fat of the sin offering he shall burn upon the altar. And he who lets the goat go to Azazel shall wash his clothes and bathe his body in water, and afterward he may come into the camp. And the bull for the sin offering and the goat for the sin offering, whose blood was brought in to make atonement in the holy place, shall be carried forth outside the camp; their skin and their flesh and their dung shall be burned with fire. And he who burns them shall wash his clothes and bathe his body in water, and afterward he may come into the camp.'

RESPONSORY   Heb 9:11,12,24

R̸ Christ, the high priest of all the blessings which were to come, has entered the sanctuary once and for all,* taking with him not the blood of goats and calves, but his own blood, having won an eternal redemption for us.

V̸ The sanctuary into which Jesus has entered is not one made by human hands; he has entered heaven itself,* taking with him . . .

THE SECOND READING   Hom 9,5.10
A reading from the homilies of Origen on the book
of Leviticus

Christ the priest, Christ our propitiation

Once a year the high priest leaves the people and goes into that
place where is the mercy seat, and over the mercy seat the
cherubim, where the ark of the covenant is kept, where stands
the altar of incense; which no one is allowed to enter except
the high priest alone.

Let me turn now to my true high priest, the Lord Jesus
Christ. When he was in the flesh he was with the people the
whole year, the year of which he himself said: 'He has sent
me to preach good news to the poor, and to proclaim the
acceptable year of the Lord and the day of forgiveness.'
Notice how only once in that year, on the day of atonement, he
enters the holy of holies, that is, he enters heaven, having
accomplished his work, and appears before the Father to make
him look with mercy on the human race, and to intercede for
all who believe in him.

The apostle John, aware of this atoning sacrifice by which
he makes propitiation for men before the Father, writes: 'My
little children, I am writing this to you so we may not sin. But
if we do sin, we have an advocate with the Father, Jesus
Christ the righteous, and he is the expiation for our sins.'

Paul similarly recalls this propitiation when he says of
Christ: 'God put him forward as an expiation by his blood, to
be received by faith.' Thus the day of atonement remains with
us until the end of the world.

Holy scripture says: 'He shall put incense on the fire
before the Lord, that the cloud of incense may cover the
mercy seat which is upon the testimony, lest he die; and he
shall take some of the blood of the bull, and sprinkle it with his
finger on the front of the mercy seat towards the east.'

This taught the ancients how the rite of propitiation which

was offered to God on behalf of men was to be carried out. But you who have turned to Christ, the true high priest, who by means of his blood obtained God's mercy for you and reconciled you with the Father, must not be content with the blood of animal flesh. Become acquainted rather with the blood of the Word, and listen to him telling you himself: 'This is my blood which will be poured out for the forgiveness of sins.'

However, do not consider pointless the words, that he 'sprinkles the blood towards the east'. Your propitiation came from the east. From there came the man whose name is the Dawn, who became the mediator between God and man.

This invites you to keep looking to the east, where the sun of righteousness rises for you, where light is always dawning for you; so that you may never walk in darkness, nor the last day find you in darkness; so that the black night of ignorance may not creep up on you; but that you may always walk in the clear light of knowledge, always have the day-light of faith, and always obtain the light of charity and peace.

RESPONSORY   Heb 6:20;7:2,3
℟ Jesus has entered heaven before us and on our behalf, a lamb without blemish;* he has become high priest of the order of Melchizedek, for ever and ever.
℣ He is the King of Righteousness, whose descendants will have no end.* He has become high priest . . .

TUESDAY

℣ Behold, now is the favourable time.
℟ This is the day of salvation.

THE FIRST READING   Lev 19:1-18,31-37
A reading from the book of Leviticus

Love your neighbour as yourself

The Lord said to Moses, 'Say to all the congregation of the people of Israel, You shall be holy; for I the Lord your God am holy. Every one of you shall revere his mother and his father, and you shall keep my sabbaths: I am the Lord your God. Do not turn to idols or make for yourselves molten gods: I am the Lord your God.

'When you offer a sacrifice of peace offerings to the Lord, you shall offer it so that you may be accepted. It shall be eaten the same day you offer it, or on the morrow; and anything left over until the third day shall be burned with fire. If it is eaten at all on the third day, it is an abomination; it will not be accepted, and every one who eats it shall bear his iniquity, because he has profaned a holy thing of the Lord; and that person shall be cut off from his people.

'When you reap the harvest of your land, you shall not reap your field to its very border, neither shall you gather the gleanings after your harvest. And you shall not strip your vineyard bare, neither shall you gather the fallen grapes of your vineyard; you shall leave them for the poor and for the sojourner: I am the Lord your God.

'You shall not steal, nor deal falsely, nor lie to one another. And you shall not swear by my name falsely, and so profane the name of your God: I am the Lord.

'You shall not oppress your neighbour or rob him. The wages of a hired servant shall not remain with you all night until the morning. You shall not curse the deaf or put a stumbling block before the blind, but you shall fear your God: I am the Lord.

'You shall do no injustice in judgment; you shall not be partial to the poor or defer to the great, but in righteousness shall you judge your neighbour. You shall not go up and down as a slanderer among your people, and you shall not stand forth against the life of your neighbour: I am the Lord.

'You shall not hate your brother in your heart, but you shall reason with your neighbour, lest you bear sin because of him. You shall not take vengeance or bear any grudge against the sons of your own people, but you shall love your neighbour as yourself: I am the Lord.

'Do not turn to mediums or wizards; do not seek them out, to be defiled by them: I am the Lord your God.

'You shall rise up before the hoary head, and honour the face of an old man, and you shall fear your God: I am the Lord.

'When a stranger sojourns with you in your land, you shall not do him wrong. The stranger who sojourns with you shall be to you as the native among you, and you shall love him as yourself; for you were strangers in the land of Egypt: I am the Lord your God.

'You shall do no wrong in judgment, in measures of length or weight or quantity. You shall have just balances, just weights, a just ephah, and a just hin: I am the Lord your God, who brought you out of the land of Egypt. And you shall observe all my statutes and all my ordinances, and do them: I am the Lord.'

RESPONSORY   Gal 5:14,13;Jn 13:34
℟ The whole of the law is summarized in a single command: Love your neighbour as yourself;* serve one another in a spirit of love.

WEEK 4: TUESDAY

℣ I give you a new commandment: love one another. Just as I have loved you, you also must love one another.* Serve one another in a spirit of love.

THE SECOND READING   Sermon 10 on Lent, 3-5
   A reading from the sermons of Pope St Leo the Great

The virtue of charity

In John's gospel the Lord says: 'By this all men will know that you are my disciples, if you have love for one another,' and in the letter of the same apostle we read: 'Beloved, let us love one another, for love is of God, and he who loves is born of God and knows God; he who does not love does not know God, for God is love.'

Let the faithful, therefore, examine their minds and subject the inmost thoughts of their hearts to a true scrutiny. If they find stored within their consciences anything of the fruits of charity, let them not doubt that God dwells in them; and in order that they may be more and more ready to receive such a guest, let them abound still more in works of unfailing compassion.

For if God is love, charity must have no limit because God cannot be confined within any bounds.

And so, beloved, although any time is suitable for the exercise of the virtue of charity, it is more especially urged on us by this present season. Thus, those who long to receive the Lord's Pasch with bodies and souls made holy must strive earnestly to acquire this grace which includes the sum of all the virtues and covers a multitude of sins.

Therefore, as we are about to celebrate that most eminent of all mysteries, in which the blood of Jesus Christ has wiped away all our sins, let us first of all prepare to offer the sacrifice of mercy; so that what we have been given by the goodness of God we may ourselves show to those who have trespassed against us.

We must show more liberal bounty towards the poor and those who suffer from all kinds of affliction in order that many voices may give thanks to God, and that the relief of those in need may support our fasts. Indeed, no other devotion of the faithful is more pleasing to the Lord than that which is directed towards his poor. Where he finds merciful concern he recognizes the reflection of his own kindness.

Let no one fear the failure of his wealth by such payments, for liberality itself is a great fortune, nor can one lack the means to practise that generosity whereby Christ feeds others and is himself fed in them. In all this work his hand intervenes to increase the quantity of bread as it is broken, and multiply it as it is distributed.

Let the almsgiver feel happy and secure, for he will have the greatest gain if he has saved the smallest amount for himself; as the blessed apostle Paul says: 'He who supplies seed to the sower will both supply bread for food and will multiply your seed and increase the harvest of your righteousness' in Christ Jesus our Lord, who lives and reigns with the Father and the Holy Spirit for ever and ever. Amen.

RESPONSORY   Lk 6:38; Col 3:13
℟ Give, and gifts will be yours;* good measure, pressed down and shaken up and running over, will be poured into your lap.
℣ You must forgive as the Lord forgave you.* Good measure, pressed down and shaken up . . .

WEDNESDAY

℣ Repent, and do penance.
℟ Make yourselves a new heart and a new spirit.

THE FIRST READING   Num 11:4-6,10-30
A reading from the book of Numbers

The Spirit is poured out on the elders and on Joshua

Now the rabble that was among them had a strong craving; and the people of Israel also wept again, and said, 'O that we had meat to eat! We remember the fish we ate in Egypt for nothing, the cucumbers, the melons, the leeks, the onions, and the garlic; but now our strength is dried up, and there is nothing at all but this manna to look at.'

Moses heard the people weeping throughout their families, every man at the door of his tent; and the anger of the Lord blazed hotly, and Moses was displeased. Moses said to the Lord, 'Why have you dealt ill with your servant? And why have I not found favour in your sight, that you lay the burden of all this people upon me? Did I conceive all this people? Did I bring them forth, that you should say to me, "Carry them in your bosom, as a nurse carries the sucking child," to the land which you did swear to give their fathers? Where am I to get meat to give to all this people? For they weep before me and say, "Give us meat, that we may eat." I am not able to carry all this people alone, the burden is too heavy for me. If you will deal thus with me, kill me at once, if I find favour in your sight, that I may not see my wretchedness.'

And the Lord said to Moses, 'Gather for me seventy men of the elders of Israel, whom you know to be the elders of the people and officers over them; and bring them to the tent of meeting, and let them take their stand there with you. And I will come down and talk with you there; and I will take some of the spirit which is upon you and put it upon them; and they shall bear the burden of the people with you, that you may not bear it yourself alone. And say to the people, "Consecrate yourselves for tomorrow, and you shall eat meat; for you have wept in the hearing of the Lord, saying, 'Who will give us meat to eat? For it was well with us in Egypt.' Therefore the Lord will give you meat, and you shall eat. You shall not eat one day, or two days, or five days, or ten days, or twenty days, but a whole month, until it comes out at your nostrils and becomes loathsome to you, because you have rejected the Lord who is among you, and have wept before him, saying, 'Why did we come forth out of Egypt?' " ' But Moses said, 'The people among whom I am number six hundred thousand on foot; and you have said, "I will give them meat, that they may eat a whole month!" Shall flocks and herds be slaughtered for them, to suffice them? Or shall all the fish of the sea be gathered together for them, to suffice them?' And the Lord said to Moses, 'Is the Lord's hand shortened? Now you shall see whether my word will come true for you or not.'

So Moses went out and told the people the words of the Lord; and he gathered seventy men of the elders of the people, and placed them round about the tent. Then the Lord came down in the cloud and spoke to him, and took some of the spirit that was upon him and put it upon the seventy elders; and when the spirit rested upon them, they prophesied. But they did so no more.

Now two men remained in the camp, one named Eldad, and the other named Medad, and the spirit rested upon them; they were among those registered, but they had not gone out to the tent, and so they prophesied in the camp. And a young man ran and told Moses, 'Eldad and Medad are prophesying in the camp.' And Joshua the son of Nun, the minister of Moses, one of his chosen men, said, 'My lord Moses, forbid them.' But Moses said to him, 'Are you jealous for my sake?

Would that all the Lord's people were prophets, that the Lord would put his spirit upon them!' And Moses and the elders of Israel returned to the camp.

RESPONSORY   Joel 2:28-29;Acts 1:8

℟ I will pour out my spirit on all mankind. Your sons and daughters shall prophesy;* I will pour out my spirit in those days.

℣ You will be filled with power when the Holy Spirit comes on you, and you will be witnesses for me to the ends of the earth.* I will pour out my spirit in those days.

THE SECOND READING   Letter 11

A reading from the letters of St Maximus the
Confessor

God's mercy towards the penitent

The heralds of the truth and ministers of divine grace, who have explained to us from the beginning right down to our own time each in his own day the saving will of God, say that nothing is so dear and loved by him as when men turn to him with true repentance.

Wishing to show that this is by far the most holy thing of all, the Divine Word of God the Father (the supreme and only revelation of infinite goodness) deigned to dwell with us in the flesh, humbling himself in a way no words can explain. He said, he did, and he suffered those things which were necessary to reconcile us, while we were yet enemies, with God the Father, and to call us back again to the life of blessedness from which we had been alienated. Not only did he heal our diseases with his miracles, and take away our infirmities by his sufferings, and, though sinless, pay our debt for us by his death like a guilty man. It was also his desire that we should aim to become like himself in love of men and in perfect mutual charity, and he taught us this in many ways.

He taught it when he proclaimed, 'I came not to call the righteous but sinners, to repentance.' And again, 'Those who are well have no need of a physician, but those who are sick.' He also said that he had come to seek and to save the lost sheep; and on another occasion, that he had been sent to the lost sheep of the house of Israel. In the same way, in the parable of the lost coin, he referred in a symbolic way to the fact that he had come to restore in men the royal likeness which had been lost by the evil-smelling filthiness of passions. Likewise, he said: 'Just so, I tell you, there is joy in heaven over one sinner who repents.'

He taught it when he brought relief, with oil, wine and bandages, to the man who had fallen among thieves and had been stripped of all his clothing and left half-dead from his injuries. Having placed him on his own beast, he entrusted him to the innkeeper; after paying what was needed for his care, he promised that when he came back he would repay whatever more was spent.

He taught it when he said that the prodigal son's all-loving father took pity on him and, kissing him as he came running back repentant, clothed him once more with the beauty of his glory, and did not reproach him in any way for what he had done.

He taught it when he found the sheep which had strayed from the divine flock of a hundred, wandering over hills and mountains. He did not drive it or beat it but brought it back to the fold. In his mercy, placing it on his shoulders, he restored it, with compassion, unharmed to the rest of the flock.

He taught it when he cried, 'Come to me all who labour and are heavy laden and I will give you rest,' and 'Take my yoke upon you.' By 'yoke' of course he meant 'commandments' or a life lived according to the principles of the gospel; by 'burden' he meant the labour which repentance seems to involve. 'For my yoke,' he says, 'is easy and my burden light.'

Again teaching divine righteousness and goodness he commanded, 'Be holy, be perfect, be merciful as your heavenly

Father is merciful,' and, 'Forgive and it shall be forgiven you' and 'whatever you wish that men would do to you, do so to them.'

RESPONSORY   Cf Ez 33:11;Ps 93:19

℟ I should have suffered anguish had I not experienced your mercy, Lord. It was you who said, I take no pleasure in the death of a sinner, but desire that he turn from his way and live;* it was you who called the Canaanite woman and the publican to repentance.

℣ When cares increased in my heart, your consolation calmed my soul.* It was you who called the Canaanite woman and the publican to repentance.

THURSDAY

℣ Happy is the man who ponders the law of the Lord.
℟ He will bring forth fruit in due season.

THE FIRST READING   Num 12:16-13:3,17-33
A reading from the book of Numbers

An advance party is sent into the promised land

The people set out from Hazeroth, and encamped in the wilderness of Paran.

The Lord said to Moses, 'Send men to spy out the land of Canaan, which I give to the people of Israel; from each tribe of their fathers shall you send a man, every one a leader among them.' So Moses sent them from the wilderness of Paran, according to the command of the Lord, all of them men who were heads of the people of Israel.

Moses sent them to spy out the land of Canaan, and said to

them, 'Go up into the Negeb yonder, and go up into the hill country, and see what the land is, and whether the people who dwell in it are strong or weak, whether they are few or many, and whether the land that they dwell in is good or bad, and whether the cities that they dwell in are camps or strongholds, and whether the land is rich or poor, and whether there is wood in it or not. Be of good courage, and bring some of the fruit of the land.' Now the time was the season of the first ripe grapes.

So they went up and spied out the land from the wilderness of Zin to Rehob, near the entrance of Hamath. They went up into the Negeb, and came to Hebron; and Ahiman, Sheshai, and Talmai, the descendants of Anak, were there. (Hebron was built seven years before Zoan in Egypt.) And they came to the Valley of Eshcol, and cut down from there a branch with a single cluster of grapes, and they carried it on a pole between two of them; they brought also some pomegranates and figs. That place was called the Valley of Eshcol, because of the cluster which the men of Israel cut down from there.

At the end of forty days they returned from spying out the land. And they came to Moses and Aaron and to all the congregation of the people of Israel in the wilderness of Paran, at Kadesh; they brought back word to them and to all the congregation, and showed them the fruit of the land. And they told him, 'We came to the land to which you sent us; it flows with milk and honey, and this is its fruit. Yet the people who dwell in the land are strong, and the cities are fortified and very large; and besides, we saw the descendants of Anak there. The Amalekites dwell in the land of the Negeb; the Hittites, the Jebusites, and the Amorites dwell in the hill country; and the Canaanites dwell by the sea, and along the Jordan.'

But Caleb quieted the people before Moses, and said, 'Let us go up at once, and occupy it; for we are well able to overcome it.' Then the men who had gone up with him said, 'We are not able to go up against the people; for they are stronger than we.' So they brought to the people of Israel an evil report of the land which they had spied out, saying, 'The land, through which we have gone, to spy it out, is a land that devours its inhabitants; and all the people that we saw in it are men of great stature. And there we saw the Nephilim (the sons of Anak, who come from the Nephilim); and we seemed to ourselves like grasshoppers, and so we seemed to them.'

RESPONSORY   Deut 1:31,32,26

℟ The Lord your God carried you all the way in the wilderness as a father carries his son, and yet* you would not trust the Lord your God.
℣ You refused to go up into the land of promise, and you rebelled against the voice of the Lord your God.* You would not trust the Lord your God.

THE SECOND READING   Sermon 15 on the Passion, 3-4
    A reading from the sermons of Pope St Leo the Great

The contemplation of the Lord's passion

Anyone who has a true devotion to the passion of the Lord must so contemplate Jesus on the cross with the eyes of his heart that Jesus' flesh is his own.

Let earth tremble at the torments of its Redeemer, let the rocks of faithless hearts be split, and, now that the mighty obstacles have been shattered, let those leap forth who were weighed down by the tombs of mortality. May signs of the future resurrection appear now in the holy city, that is, the Church of God, and hearts experience that which our bodies will undergo.

The victory of the cross is denied to none of the weak; there is no man who cannot be helped by the prayer of Christ. For if his prayer aided the multitudes who raged against him, how much more does it help those who turn to him?

Ignorance has been taken away, difficulties have been made easier, and the sacred blood of Christ has extinguished the flaming sword which blocked the way to life. The darkness of the former night has given way to the true light.

The Christian people are invited to share the riches of paradise, and the road back to the fatherland they lost has been thrown open once more to all who have been reborn, unless anyone closes for himself that way which the faith of the thief was able to open up.

The activities of this present life must not fill us with anxiety or pride, so that we do not strive with all the powers of our soul to be conformed to our Redeemer in the way that he showed us. He performed and suffered everything necessary for our salvation, so that the power which was in the head might also be found in the body.

Indeed, what man was left deprived of his mercy, except the unbeliever, by that taking of our substance in the divinity, whereby 'The Word was made flesh and dwelt among us'? Who does not share a common nature with Christ if he has accepted him who assumed our humanity, and has been born by that Spirit by which he was begotten? Again, who would not recognize his own infirmities in him? Who would be unable to see that taking food, resting in sleep, being troubled by grief, and weeping out of love, are the marks of the form of a servant?

Because humanity needed to be cured of its ancient wounds and cleansed of the filth of sin, the only-begotten Son of God became the son of man too, lacking nothing of the reality of manhood and nothing of the fulness of divinity.

That belongs to us which lay lifeless in the tomb, rose again on the third day, and ascended above all the heights of heaven to the right hand of the glory of the Father. If we follow the way of his commandments, and are not ashamed to confess how great a price he paid for our salvation, in bodily humility, we too shall come to share in his glory. For what he predicted shall be fulfilled clearly, 'Everyone who acknowledges me before men, I also will acknowledge before my Father who is in heaven.'

RESPONSORY   1 Cor 1:18,23
℟ To those who court their own ruin, the message of the cross
is but folly;* to us, who are on the way to salvation, it is
evidence of God's power.
℣ What we preach is Christ crucified, to the Jews a dis-
couragement, to the Gentiles, mere folly;* to us, who are on
the way to salvation, it is evidence of God's power.

FRIDAY

℣ Return to the Lord, your God.
℟ For he is gracious and merciful.

THE FIRST READING   Num 14:1-25
A reading from the book of Numbers

The people murmur and Moses intercedes for them

All the congregation raised a loud cry; and the people wept
that night. And all the people of Israel murmured against
Moses and Aaron; the whole congregation said to them,
'Would that we had died in the land of Egypt! Or would that
we had died in this wilderness! Why does the Lord bring us
into this land, to fall by the sword? Our wives and our little
ones will become a prey; would it not be better for us to go
back to Egypt?'
And they said to one another, 'Let us choose a captain, and
go back to Egypt.' Then Moses and Aaron fell on their faces
before all the assembly of the congregation of the people of
Israel. And Joshua the son of Nun and Caleb the son of
Jephunneh, who were among those who had spied out the
land, rent their clothes, and said to all the congregation of the
people of Israel, 'The land, which we passed through to spy it

out, is an exceedingly good land. If the Lord delights in us, he will bring us into this land and give it to us, a land which flows with milk and honey. Only, do not rebel against the Lord; and do not fear the people of the land, for they are bread for us; their protection is removed from them, and the Lord is with us; do not fear them.' But all the congregation said to stone them with stones.

Then the glory of the Lord appeared at the tent of meeting to all the people of Israel. And the Lord said to Moses, 'How long will this people despise me? And how long will they not believe in me, in spite of all the signs which I have wrought among them? I will strike them with the pestilence and dis-inherit them, and I will make of you a nation greater and mightier than they.'

But Moses said to the Lord, 'Then the Egyptians will hear of it, for you brought up this people in your might from among them, and they will tell the inhabitants of this land. They have heard that you, O Lord, are in the midst of this people; for you, O Lord, are seen face to face, and your cloud stands over them and you go before them, in a pillar of cloud by day and in a pillar of fire by night. Now if you kill this people as one man, then the nations who have heard your fame will say, "Because the Lord was not able to bring this people into the land which he swore to give to them, therefore he has slain them in the wilderness." And now, I pray you, let the power of the Lord be great as you have promised, saying, "The Lord is slow to anger, and abounding in steadfast love, for-giving iniquity, and transgression but he will by no means clear the guilty, visiting the iniquity of fathers upon children, upon the third and upon the fourth generation." Pardon the iniquity of this people, I pray you, according to the greatness of your steadfast love, and according as you have forgiven this people, from Egypt even until now.'

Then the Lord said, 'I have pardoned, according to your word; but truly, as I live, and as all the earth shall be filled with the glory of the Lord, none of the men who have seen my glory and my signs which I wrought in Egypt and in the wilderness, and yet have put me to the proof these ten times and have not hearkened to my voice, shall see the land which I swore to give to their fathers; and none of those who despised me shall see it. But my servant Caleb, because he has a different spirit and has followed me fully, I will bring into the land into which he went, and his descendants shall possess it. Now, since the Amalekites and the Canaanites dwell in the valleys, turn tomorrow and set out for the wilderness by the way to the Red Sea.'

RESPONSORY   Ps 102:8,9,13,14

℟ The Lord is compassion and love, slow to anger and rich in mercy; his wrath will come to an end; he will not be angry for ever.* As a father has compassion on his children, the Lord has pity on those who fear him.

℣ He knows the stuff we are made of, he remembers that we are dust.* As a father has compassion . . .

THE SECOND READING   Letter 5,1-2
    A reading from the Easter letters of St Athanasius

The Easter mystery makes those who are separated in the body, spiritually close

It is an excellent thing, brothers, to go from one feast to another, to pass from one prayer to another, to advance from the keeping of one feast or solemnity to another. We are very near now to that time which is for us a new beginning, the commencement of the blessed Passover in which the Lord was sacrificed. We feed as on the food of life, and with his precious blood as from a fountain we always delight our souls. Nevertheless, our thirst and burning desire are never satisfied. But our Saviour is ready for those who are thirsty, and for his love he brings to this festival day those who thirst in their hearts, as he himself, our Saviour, told us, 'If anyone thirsts, let him come to me and drink.'

Not only then did he satisfy a man's thirst when anyone approached; but each time anyone asks, access to the Saviour is freely granted. The grace that comes from this feast is not restricted to one occasion, nor does its radiant splendour die away, but it is always available to illuminate the minds of those who long for it. It is a source of continual power for those whose minds are enlightened, and who study the scriptures day and night, like that man who is called blessed in the sacred psalm which says, 'Blessed is the man who walks not in the counsel of the wicked, nor stands in the way of sinners, nor sits in the seat of scoffers; but his delight is in the law of the Lord, and on his law he meditates day and night.'

Now, that God who first instituted this feast for us, my beloved, has also permitted us to celebrate it each year. He who handed over his Son to death for our salvation, for the same reason gives us this holy feast which is recalled annually. This feast guides us through the misfortunes which befall us in this world. And now God gives us the happiness of salvation, which flows from this feast, and makes us friends. At the same time, he gathers us all together, uniting us spiritually wherever we may be, letting us pray in common and offer common thanksgiving, as is proper on a feast day. The miracle of his kindness lies in this: he brings together to this feast those who are far off; and those who are perhaps separated in the body, he makes spiritually close by the unity of faith.

RESPONSORY   Zeph 3:8,9;Jn 12:32
R̷ Wait for me, says the Lord, for the day when I arise.* At that time I will change the speech of the peoples to a pure speech, that all of them may call on the name of the Lord and serve him with one accord.
V̷ I shall draw all men to myself, when I am lifted up from the earth.* At that time I will change the speech . . .

SATURDAY

℣ The man who lives by the truth comes into the light.
℟ So that his good works may be seen.

THE FIRST READING   Num 20:1-13;21:4-9
A reading from the book of Numbers

The waters of Meribah. The bronze serpent

The people of Israel, the whole congregation, came into the
wilderness of Zin in the first month, and the people stayed in
Kadesh; and Miriam died there, and was buried there.

Now there was no water for the congregation and they
assembled themselves together against Moses and against
Aaron. And the people contended with Moses, and said,
'Would that we had died when our brethren died before the
Lord! Why have you brought the assembly of the Lord into
this wilderness, that we should die here, both we and our
cattle? And why have you made us come up out of Egypt, to
bring us to this evil place? It is no place for grain, or figs, or
vines, or pomegranates; and there is no water to drink.'

Then Moses and Aaron went from the presence of the
assembly to the door of the tent of meeting, and fell on their
faces. And the glory of the Lord appeared to them, and the
Lord said to Moses, 'Take the rod, and assemble the congregation, you and Aaron your brother, and tell the rock before
their eyes to yield its water; so you shall bring water out of the
rock for them; so you shall give drink to the congregation and
their cattle.' And Moses took the rod from before the Lord, as
he commanded him.

And Moses and Aaron gathered the assembly together
before the rock, and he said to them, 'Hear now, you rebels;

shall we bring forth water for you out of this rock?' And Moses lifted up his hand and struck the rock with his rod twice; and water came forth abundantly, and the congregation drank, and their cattle. And the Lord said to Moses and Aaron, 'Because you did not believe in me, to sanctify me in the eyes of the people of Israel, therefore you shall not bring this assembly into the land which I have given them.' These are the waters of Meribah, where the people of Israel contended with the Lord, and he showed himself holy among them.

From Mount Hor they set out by the way to the Red Sea, to go around the land of Edom; and the people became impatient on the way. And the people spoke against God and against Moses, 'Why have you brought us up out of Egypt to die in the wilderness? For there is no food and no water, and we loathe this worthless food.' Then the Lord sent fiery serpents among the people, and they bit the people, so that many people of Israel died. And the people came to Moses, and said, 'We have sinned, for we have spoken against the Lord and against you; pray to the Lord, that he take away the serpents from us.' So Moses prayed for the people. And the Lord said to Moses, 'Make a fiery serpent, and set it on a pole; and every one who is bitten, when he sees it, shall live.' So Moses made a bronze serpent, and set it on a pole; and if a serpent bit any man, he would look at the bronze serpent and live.

RESPONSORY   Jn 3:14,15,17

℟ The Son of Man must be lifted up as Moses lifted up the serpent in the desert,* so that everyone who believes may have eternal life in him.

℣ God sent his Son into the world, not to condemn the world, but so that through him the world might be saved,* so that everyone who believes . . .

A reading from the Constitution of the Second Vatican
Council on the Church in the Modern World

All human activity will be purified in the paschal mystery

Sacred scripture teaches mankind what has also been con-
firmed by man's own experience, namely that the great
advantages of human progress are fraught with grave temptations: the hierarchy of values has been disordered, good and
evil intermingle, and every man and every group is interested
only in its own affairs, not in those of others.

So it is that the earth has not yet become the scene of true
brotherhood; rather, at the present time man's enormous
power threatens to put an end to the human race itself.

To the question of how this unhappy situation can be overcome, Christians reply that all these human activities, which
are daily endangered by pride and inordinate self-love, must
be purified and perfected by the cross and resurrection of
Christ.

Redeemed by Christ and made a new creature by the Holy
Spirit man can, indeed he must, love the things of God's
creation: it is from God that he has received them and it is as
flowing from God's hand that he looks upon them and
reveres them.

Man thanks his divine benefactor for all these things, he
uses them and enjoys them in a spirit of poverty and freedom:
thus he is brought to a true possession of the world, as having
nothing yet possessing everything: 'All things are yours; and
you are Christ's; and Christ is God's.

The Word of God, through whom all things were made,
became man and dwelt among men: a perfect man, he entered
world history, taking that history into himself and recapitulat-
ing it. He reveals to us that 'God is love' and at the same time
teaches that the fundamental law of human perfection, and

consequently of the transformation of the world, is the new commandment of love.

He assures those who trust in the charity of God that the way of love is open to all men and that the effort to establish a universal brotherhood will not be in vain. This love is not something reserved for important matters, but must be exercised above all in the ordinary circumstances of daily life.

Christ's example in dying for us sinners teaches us that we must carry the cross, which the flesh and the world inflict on the shoulders of all who seek after justice and peace.

Constituted Lord by his resurrection and possessing all authority in heaven and on earth, Christ is now at work in the hearts of men by the power of his Spirit; not only does he arouse in them a desire for the world to come but he invigorates, purifies, and strengthens the generous aspirations of mankind to make life more humane and conquer the earth for this purpose.

The gifts of the Spirit are diverse: some men are called to testify openly to mankind's yearning for its heavenly home and keep the awareness of it vividly before men's minds; others are called to dedicate themselves to the service of men and in this way to prepare the way for the kingdom of heaven. But the Spirit brings freedom to all men, who are ready to put aside love of self and integrate earthly resources into human life, in order to reach out to that future day when mankind itself will become an offering accepted by God.

RESPONSORY   2 Cor 5:15;Rom 4:25

℟ Christ died for all,* so that living men should live no longer for themselves, but for him who died and was raised to life for them.
℣ He was put to death for our sins and raised to life to justify us,* so that living men . . .

WEEK 5: SUNDAY

℣ If any man is faithful to my word.
℞ He will never see death.

THE FIRST READING   Heb 1:1-2:4
          A reading from the letter to the Hebrews

> *The Son is to inherit everything and is exalted above the*
> *angels*

At various times in the past and in various different ways,
God spoke to our ancestors through the prophets; but in our
own time, the last days, he has spoken to us through his Son,
the Son that he has appointed to inherit everything and
through whom he made everything there is. He is the radiant
light of God's glory and the perfect copy of his nature, sustaining the universe by his powerful command; and now that
he has destroyed the defilement of sin, he has gone to take his
place in heaven at the right hand of divine Majesty. So he is
now as far above the angels as the title which he has inherited
is higher than their own name.

God has never said to any angel: 'You are my Son, today I
have become your father,' or: 'I will be a father to him and he
a son to me.' Again, when he brings the First-born into the
world, he says: 'Let all the angels of God worship him.'
About the angels, he says: 'He makes his angels winds and his
servants flames of fire,' but to his Son he says: 'God, your
throne shall last for ever and ever'; and: 'his royal sceptre is
the sceptre of virtue; virtue you love as much as you hate
wickedness. This is why God, your God, has anointed you
with the oil of gladness, above all your rivals.' And again: 'It
is you, Lord, who laid earth's foundations in the beginning,

the heavens are the work of your hands; all will vanish, though you remain, all wear out like a garment; you will roll them up like a cloak, and like a garment they will be changed. But yourself, you never change and your years are unending.' God has never said to any angel: 'Sit at my right hand and I will make your enemies a footstool for you.' The truth is they are all spirits whose work is service, sent to help those who will be the heirs of salvation.

We ought, then, to turn our minds more attentively than before to what we have been taught, so that we do not drift away. If a promise that was made through angels proved to be so true that every infringement and disobedience brought its own proper punishment, then we shall certainly not go un-punished if we neglect this salvation that is promised to us. The promise was first announced by the Lord himself, and is guaranteed to us by those who heard him; God himself con-firmed their witness with signs and marvels and miracles of all kinds, and by freely giving the gifts of the Holy Spirit.

RESPONSORY   Heb 1:3;12:2

℟ Christ Jesus is the radiant light of the Father's glory and the perfect copy of his nature, sustaining the universe by his powerful command;* now that he has made atonement for sin, he has gone to take his place at the right hand of the divine Majesty.

℣ Jesus, who leads us in our faith and brings it to perfection, for the sake of the joy which was still in the future, endured the cross;* now that he has made atonement for sin . . .

THE SECOND READING   Letter 14,1-2
    A reading from the Easter letters of St Athanasius

We keep the Lord's feast which is coming, not in word but in action

The Word is very close to us, the Word who has become all things for us, our Lord Jesus Christ, who promises to remain

133

with us always. And so he proclaims: 'Lo, I am with you all the days of the world.' As he is the shepherd, the high priest, the way and the door, and has become all things at once for us, so he has appeared as our feast and our solemnity also: the blessed Apostle says: 'Our pasch has been sacrificed, Christ himself,' who was awaited. He looked with favour on the psalmist who prayed: 'My joy, rescue me from those who surround me.' This is the true joy, this is the real solemnity: freedom from evil. If anyone wishes to attain this, he must be of blameless life and reflect in his soul in the quiet of the fear of the Lord.

Thus the saints rejoiced all their lives long, like men at a feast. One of them, the blessed David, used to rise during the night not once but seven times and honour God in prayer. Another, the great Moses, would express his joy in canticles and sing psalms for the victory over Pharaoh and over those who had kept the Hebrews in toil and oppression. Finally there were others who carried out the sacred liturgy with cheerful constancy, such as the great Samuel and the renowned Elias. By the quality of their lives they have won freedom and now they celebrate a feast in heaven; they rejoice after their former pilgrimage in the shadow and now distinguish the truth from what was only a figure.

We are now observing a solemn feast—which way are we to take? As we draw near to this day of celebration—whom shall we have as leader? No one, dearly beloved, except him whom you will name with me our Lord Jesus Christ, who said: 'I am the way.' He it is, as Saint John says, who takes away the sin of the world. He purifies our souls—as Jeremiah the prophet says: 'Stand on the ways and see and discern which is the right way and on it you will find cleansing for your souls.'

In the past the blood of goats and the ashes of a calf sprinkled over the unclean could only purify the body; now through the grace of the Word of God each and everyone is cleansed to the full. If we follow close behind him, we shall be permitted to

134

contemplate that eternal feast even here in anticipation, as if we were standing in the courts of the heavenly Jerusalem— just as the blessed apostles, who followed the Saviour as their leader, and were then and are still now teachers of a like grace, for they said: 'Lo, we have left everything and have followed you.' For we follow the Lord, and we keep the Lord's feast not only in word but in action.

RESPONSORY   Cf Heb 6:60; Jn 1:29
℟ Jesus has entered heaven before us and on our behalf, a lamb without blemish;* he has become high priest of the order of Melchizedek, for ever and ever.
℣ Look, there is the Lamb of God; it is he who takes away the sin of the world.* He has become high priest of the order of Melchizedek, for ever and ever.

MONDAY

℣ Repent, and believe in the gospel.
℟ The kingdom of God is at hand.

THE FIRST READING   Heb 2:5-18
   A reading from the letter to the Hebrews

Jesus is the author of our salvation, since he has become like his brothers in all things

He did not appoint angels to be rulers of the world to come, and that world is what we are talking about. Somewhere there is a passage that shows us this. It runs: 'What is man that you should spare a thought for him, the son of man that you should care for him? For a short while you made him lower than the angels; you crowned him with glory and splendour. You have put him in command of everything.' Well then, if he has 'put him in command of everything,' he has left nothing which is not under his command. At present, it is true, we are not able to see that 'everything has been put under his command', but we do see in Jesus one who was 'for a short while made lower than the angels' and is now 'crowned with glory and splendour' because he submitted to death; by God's grace he had to experience death for all mankind.

As it was his purpose to bring a great many of his sons into glory, it was appropriate that God, for whom everything exists and through whom everything exists, should make perfect, through suffering, the leader who would take them to their salvation. For the one who sanctifies, and the ones who are sanctified, are of the same stock; that is why he openly calls them 'brothers' in the text: 'I shall announce your name to my brothers, praise you in full assembly,' or the text: 'In him I hope,' or the text: 'Here I am with the children whom God has given me.'

Since all the children share the same blood and flesh, he too shared equally in it, so that by his death he could take away all the power of the devil, who had power over death, and set free all those who had been held in slavery all their lives by the fear of death. For it was not the angels that he took to himself; he took to himself descent from Abraham. It was essential that he should in this way become completely like his brothers so that he could be a compassionate and trustworthy high priest of God's religion, able to atone for human sins. That is, because he has himself been through temptation he is able to help others who are tempted.

RESPONSORY   Heb 2:11,17;Bar 3:38
℟. Christ who sanctifies, and the ones who are sanctified, are of the same stock; it was essential, therefore, that he should become completely like his brothers,* so that he could be a compassionate and trustworthy high priest.

℣ God appeared on earth and moved among men,* so that he could be a compassionate and trustworthy high priest.

THE SECOND READING   On Ps 129

A reading from the commentary of St John Fisher
on the Psalms

Even if someone has sinned, we have an advocate with the Father

Jesus Christ is our high priest and his precious body is our sacrifice, which he offered on the altar of the cross for the salvation of all men.

The blood, poured out for our redemption, was not that of calves or goats, as in the old law, but the blood of the most innocent lamb, Jesus Christ our Saviour.

The temple in which our high priest offered sacrifice was not man-made but was built by the power of God alone. For he poured out his blood before the eyes of the world: and this temple is the work of God's hand alone.

This temple has two parts: one is the earth on which we now dwell; the other is still unknown to us while we are mortal.

First he offered sacrifice here on earth when he underwent his most bitter death. Then, clothed with the new garment of immortality he entered the holy of holies taking his own blood, that is, he went into heaven; and there he showed forth before the throne of his heavenly Father that blood of great price which he had poured out seven times for all sinful men.

This sacrifice is so pleasing and acceptable to God that as soon as he sees it he cannot but take pity on us immediately and show mercy to all who are truly repentant.

Moreover, it is an eternal sacrifice. It is offered not just every year, as was the case among the Jews, but every day, and indeed even every hour and every moment, so that we may have the strongest possible consolation and support. That is why the Apostle adds: 'Having found an eternal redemption.'

A share in this holy, eternal sacrifice is given to all who have undertaken true contrition and penance for their sins, who have made a definite resolve not to repeat their faults for the future but to persevere steadfastly in the pursuit of virtue which they have begun.

This is affirmed by Saint John in these words: 'My little children, I am writing this to you so that you may not sin. But if anyone does sin, we have an advocate with the Father, Jesus Christ the just one: he is the propitiation for our sins, not for ours only but also for the sins of the whole world.'

RESPONSORY   Rom 5:10,8

℞ If, when we were God's enemies, we were reconciled to him through the death of his Son,* how much more, now that we are reconciled, shall we be saved by his life!

℣ Christ died for us while we were yet sinners.* How much more . . .

TUESDAY

℣ Behold, now is the favourable time.
℞ This is the day of salvation.

THE FIRST READING   Heb 3:1-19
A reading from the letter to the Hebrews

Jesus, the apostle of our religion

That is why all you who are holy brothers and have had the same heavenly call should turn your minds to Jesus, the apostle and the high priest of our religion. He was faithful to the one who appointed him, just like Moses, who stayed faithful in all his house; but he has been found to deserve a

greater glory than Moses. It is the difference between the
honour given to the man that built the house and to the house
itself. Every house is built by someone, of course; but God
built everything that exists. It is true that Moses was faithful
in the house of God, as a servant, acting as witness to the
things which were to be divulged later; but Christ was faithful
as a son, and as the master in the house. And we are his house,
as long as we cling to our hope with the confidence that we
glory in.

The Holy Spirit says: 'If only you would listen to him today;
do not harden your hearts, as happened in the Rebellion, on
the Day of Temptation in the wilderness, when your ancestors
challenged me and tested me, though they had seen what I
could do for forty years. That was why I was angry with that
generation and said: How unreliable these people who refuse
to grasp my ways! And so, in anger, I swore that not one would
reach the place of rest I had for them.' Take care, brothers,
that there is not in any one of your community a wicked mind,
so unbelieving as to turn away from the living God. Every day,
as long as this 'today' lasts, keep encouraging one another so
that none of you is hardened by the lure of sin, because we
shall remain co-heirs with Christ only if we keep a grasp on
our first confidence right to the end. In this saying: 'If only
you would listen to him today; do not harden your hearts, as
happened in the Rebellion,' those who rebelled after they had
listened were all the people who were brought out of Egypt by
Moses. And those who made God angry for forty years were
the ones who sinned and whose dead bodies were left lying in
the wilderness. Those that he swore would never reach the
place of rest he had for them were those who had been disobedient. We see, then, that it was because they were unfaith-
ful that they were not able to reach it.

RESPONSORY   Heb 3:6;Eph 2:21
℟ Christ is faithful as the Son in charge of God's house,* and
we are his house.

℣ In him the whole building is bonded together and grows into a holy temple in the Lord,* and we are his house.

THE SECOND READING   Sermon 8 on the Passion, 6-8
    A reading from the sermons of Pope St Leo the Great

> *The cross of Christ is the source of all blessings, the cause of all graces*

Let our understanding, enlightened by the Spirit of truth, take in with a pure and free spirit the glory of the cross which shines on heaven and earth. Let it see with inner vision what the Lord meant when he spoke of his impending passion: 'The hour has come for the Son of man to be glorified,' and later: 'Now my soul is troubled, and what shall I say? "Father, save me from this hour?" No, for this purpose I have come to this hour. Father, glorify your Son.' And when the voice of the Father had spoken from heaven: 'I have glorified him and I will glorify him again,' Jesus said in reply to the bystanders: 'This voice has come for your sake, not for mine. Now is the judgment of the world, now shall the ruler of this world be cast out. And I, if I am lifted up from the earth, will draw all things to myself.'

O wonderful power of the cross! O indescribable glory of the passion! There is the tribunal of the Lord, and the judgment of the world, and the power of the crucified one.

Lord, you drew all things to yourself so that all nations everywhere in their dedication to you might celebrate in a full, clear sacramental rite what was done only in the Jewish temple and in signs and shadows.

Now the order of the levites is more glorious, the dignity of the elders more exalted, and the anointing of the priests more holy: for your cross is the source of all blessings, the cause of all graces. Through it those who believe receive strength from weakness, glory from shame, life from death. Now too the diversity of the carnal sacrifices is ended and the one offering of your body and blood consummates all the different victims, for you are the true Lamb of God who take away the sins of the world. You bring all the mysteries to accomplishment in yourself so that as for all victims there is now one sacrifice, so there may be one kingdom of all peoples.

So, dearly beloved, let us acclaim what the blessed teacher of the Gentiles, the apostle Paul, gloriously acclaimed: 'The word is sure and worthy of all belief: Jesus Christ came into this world to save sinners.'

All the more wonderful is the mercy of God towards us, because Christ died not for the just or the holy but for the wicked and the impious. And though the divine nature could not admit the sting of death, by being born from us he took what he could offer for us.

In the past he threatened our death with the power of his death, speaking through the prophet Osee: 'Death, I shall be your death; Sheol, I shall be your bite.' For by dying he submitted to the laws of the underworld, but by rising again he destroyed their power; and so he broke the uninterrupted sequence of death and made temporary what was eternal. 'For as all die in Adam, so all shall live in Christ.'

RESPONSORY   Col 2:14-15;Jn 8:28

℟ Christ has done away with every record of the debt that we had to pay by nailing it to the cross;* on that cross he despoiled the cosmic powers and authorities, and boldly made a spectacle of them, leading them as captives in his triumphal procession.
℣ When you have lifted up the Son of Man on the cross, you will know that I am he.* On that cross . . .

WEDNESDAY

℣ Repent, and do penance.
℟ Make yourselves a new heart and a new spirit.

THE FIRST READING   Heb 6:9-20
A reading from the letter to the Hebrews

The faithfulness of God is our hope

My dear people—in spite of what we have just said, we are
sure you are in a better state and on the way to salvation. God
would not be so unjust as to forget all you have done, the love
that you have for his name or the services you have done, and
are still doing, for the saints. Our one desire is that every one
of you should go on showing the same earnestness to the end,
to the perfect fulfilment of our hopes, never growing careless,
but imitating those who have the faith and the perseverance to
inherit the promises.

When God made the promise to Abraham, he swore by his
own self, since it was impossible for him to swear by anyone
greater: 'I will shower blessings on you and give you many
descendants.' Because of that, Abraham persevered and saw
the promise fulfilled. Men, of course, swear an oath by something greater than themselves, and between men, confirmation
by an oath puts an end to all dispute. In the same way, when
God wanted to make the heirs to the promise thoroughly
realize that his purpose was unalterable, he conveyed this by
an oath; so that there would be two unalterable things in which
it was impossible for God to be lying, and so that we, now we
have found safety, should have a strong encouragement to
take a firm grip on the hope that is held out to us. Here we
have an anchor for our soul, as sure as it is firm, and reaching

right through beyond the veil where Jesus has entered before us and on our behalf, to become a high priest of the order of Melchizedek, and for ever.

RESPONSORY   Heb 6:19,20;7:24,25

℟ Jesus has entered through the veil before us and on our behalf, to become a high priest of the order of Melchizedek, and for ever.* He is living for ever to intercede for us.
℣ He can never lose his priesthood. It follows, then, that his power to save those who come to God through him is utterly certain.* He is living for ever to intercede for us.

THE SECOND READING   On Ps 85,1
A reading from the discourses of St Augustine
on the Psalms

Jesus Christ prays for us, prays in us, is prayed to by us

This is the greatest gift which God could give to men: he made his Word, through whom he created all things, head over them and joined them to him as his members, so that he might be Son of God and son of man, one God with the Father, one man with men. So when we turn to God in prayer, we do not separate the Son from him, and when the body of the Son prays, it does not separate its head from itself: it is the one Saviour of his body, our Lord Jesus Christ, Son of God, who prays for us and prays in us and is prayed to by us.

He prays for us as our priest; he prays in us as our head; he is prayed to by us as our God.

So we must recognize our voices in him and his voices in us. When something is said of the Lord Jesus Christ, particularly in prophecy, which would refer, as it were, to a certain lowliness unworthy of God, we must not hesitate to attribute it to him, since he did not hesitate to join himself to us. For the whole creation is at his service, since the whole creation was made through him.

Accordingly, when we behold his exaltation and his divinity, when we hear the words: 'In the beginning was the Word, and the Word was with God, and the Word was God. This was in the beginning with God. All things were made through him and, without him nothing was made,' when we behold this supreme divinity of the Son which surpasses all that is exalted in creatures, we hear him also in some part of the scriptures as it were sighing, praying, confessing.

We hesitate to attribute these words to him, because our reflection has just been contemplating him in his divinity and is slow to descend to his lowliness. It directed its words to him when it was praying to God, and now it wavers generally, as if it would be doing him a wrong to acknowledge his words as man, and it tries to change their meaning; and yet it meets with nothing in scripture except what always reverts to him, and does not allow it to turn away from him.

Let it wake up then and keep watch in its faith. Let it see that he whom it was contemplating a little earlier in the form of God took on the form of a servant; made in the likeness of man and found in human form, he humbled himself, made obedient to death; and he wished to make his own the words of the psalm, as he hung on the cross and said: 'My God, my God, why have you forsaken me?'

So he is prayed to in the form of God, he prays in the form of a servant: in the first case as creator, in the latter as created, the unchanged taking on the creature that the creature may be changed, and making us with himself one man, head and body. We pray to him, through him, in him; we speak with him, he speaks with us.

RESPONSORY   Jn 16:24,23

℟ So far you have asked nothing in my name.* Ask, and you will receive that your joy may be complete.

℣ I tell you the truth: the Father will give you anything you ask of him in my name.* Ask, and you will receive . . .

THURSDAY

℣ Happy is the man who ponders the law of the Lord.
℟ He will bring forth fruit in due season.

THE FIRST READING   Heb 7:1-10
A reading from the letter to the Hebrews

Melchizedek is the figure of the perfect priest

You remember that 'Melchizedek, king of Salem, a priest of
God Most High, went to meet Abraham who was on his way
back after defeating the kings, and blessed him'; and also that
it was to him that Abraham gave a tenth of all that he had. By
the interpretation of his name, he is, first, 'king of righteousness' and also king of Salem, that is, 'king of peace'; he has no
father, mother or ancestry, and his life has no beginning or
ending; he is like the Son of God. He remains a priest for ever.
    Now think how great this man must have been, if the
patriarch Abraham paid him a tenth of the treasure he had
captured. We know that any of the descendants of Levi who
are admitted to the priesthood are obliged by the Law to take
tithes from the people, and this is taking them from their own
brothers although they too are descended from Abraham. But
this man, who was not of the same descent, took his tenth
from Abraham, and he gave his blessing to the holder of the
promises. Now it is indisputable that a blessing is given by a
superior to an inferior. Further, in the one case it is ordinary
mortal men who receive the tithes, and in the other, someone
who is declared to be still alive. It could be said that Levi
himself, who receives tithes, actually paid them, in the person
of Abraham, because he was still in the loins of his ancestor
when Melchizedek came to meet him.

RESPONSORY   Cf Gen 14:18;Heb 7:3;
                                   cf Ps 109:4;Heb 7:16

℟ Melchizedek, king of Salem, brought out bread and wine;
he was a priest of God Most High, like the Son of God;* to
whom the Lord swore an oath: You are a priest for ever, a
priest like Melchizedek of old.
℣ The second Melchizedek is a priest not by virtue of a law
about physical descent, but by the power of an indestructible
life;* to whom the Lord swore an oath . . .

THE SECOND READING   N 9
A reading from the Constitution of the Second Vatican
Council on the Church

The Church, the visible sacrament of saving unity

'Behold the days are coming, says the Lord, when I will make
a new covenant with the house of Israel and the house of
Judah . . . I will put my law within them and I will write it
upon their hearts: I will be their God, and they shall be my
people. For they shall all know me, from the least of them
even to the greatest, says the Lord.'

Christ instituted this new covenant, that is to say, the new
testament, in his blood, by calling together a people made up
of Jew and Gentile, making them one, not according to the
flesh but the Spirit. This was to be the new People of God.

For those who believe in Christ, who are reborn not from a
perishable but from an imperishable seed through the Word
of the living God, not from flesh but from water and the Holy
Spirit, are finally established as 'a chosen race, a royal priesthood, a holy nation, a purchased people, who in times past
were not a people, but are now the people of God.'

That messianic people has Christ as its head, 'who was
delivered up for our sins and rose again for our justification,'
and now, having won a name which is above all names, reigns
in glory in heaven.

The heritage of this people is the dignity and freedom of the sons of God, in whose hearts the Holy Spirit dwells as in his temple.

Its law is the new commandment to love as Christ loved us.

Its destiny is the kingdom of God, which was begun by God himself on earth, and which is to be further extended until it is brought to perfection by him at the end of time. Then Christ, our life, will appear, and 'creation itself also will be delivered from its slavery to corruption into the freedom of the glory of the sons of God'.

So it is that this messianic people, though it does not actually include all men, and may at times look like a small flock, is nonetheless a lasting and sure seed of unity, hope, and salvation for the whole human race.

Established by Christ as a communion of life, love and truth, it is also used by him as an instrument for the redemption of all, and as the light of the world and the salt of the earth is sent forth into the whole world.

Just as Israel according to the flesh, wandering as an exile in the desert, was already called the Church of God, so the new Israel, going forward in the present world seeking a future and abiding city, is also called the Church of Christ. Indeed he has purchased it for himself with his blood, has filled it with his Spirit, and provided it with means suitable for its visible and social unity.

God has called together as one all who in faith look upon Jesus as the author of salvation and the source of unity and peace. He has established them as the Church, so that for each and all she may be the visible sacrament of this saving unity.

RESPONSORY   1 Pet 2:9,10;Ps 32:12

℟ You are a people set apart.* At one time you were not God's people, but now you are his people; at one time you did not know God's mercy, but now you have received his mercy.
℣ They are happy whose God is the Lord, the people he has chosen as his own.* At one time you were not God's people . . .

FRIDAY

THE FIRST READING   Heb 7:11-28
        A reading from the letter to the Hebrews

The everlasting priesthood of Christ

If perfection had been reached through the levitical priest-hood because the Law given to the nation rests on it, why was it still necessary for a new priesthood to arise, one of the same order as Melchizedek not counted as being of the same order as Aaron? But any change in the priesthood must mean a change in the Law as well.

So our Lord, of whom these things were said, belonged to a different tribe, the members of which have never done service at the altar; everyone knows he came from Judah, a tribe which Moses did not even mention when dealing with priests.

This becomes even more clearly evident when there appears a second Melchizedek, who is a priest not by virtue of a law about physical descent, but by the power of an indestructible life. For it was about him that the prophecy was made: 'You are a priest of the order of Melchizedek, and for ever.' The earlier commandment is thus abolished, because it was neither effective nor useful, since the Law could not make anyone perfect; but now this commandment is replaced by something better—the hope that brings us nearer to God.

What is more, this was not done without the taking of an oath. The others, indeed, were made priests without any oath; but he with an oath sworn by the one who declared to him: 'The Lord has sworn an oath which he will never retract: you are a priest, and for ever.' And it follows that it is a greater covenant for which Jesus has become our guarantee. Then there used to be a great number of those other priests, because death put an end to each one of them; but this one, because he remains for ever, can never lose his priesthood. It follows, then, that his power to save is utterly certain, since he is living for ever to intercede for all who come to God through him.

To suit us, the ideal high priest would have to be holy, innocent and uncontaminated, beyond the influence of sinners, and raised up above the heavens; one who would not need to offer sacrifices every day, as the other high priests do for their own sins and then for those of the people, because he has done this once and for all by offering himself. The Law appoints high priests who are men subject to weakness; but the promise on oath, which came after the Law, appointed the Son who is made perfect for ever.

RESPONSORY   Heb 5:5,6;7:20,21
℟ Christ did not give himself the glory of becoming high priest; he had it from the one who said to him:* You are a priest for ever, a priest like Melchizedek of old.
℣ Others were made priests without any oath, but Jesus with an oath by the one who declared to him,* You are a priest for ever . . .

THE SECOND READING   Chs 22,62
A reading from the treatise of St Fulgentius of Ruspe
To Peter on faith

He offered himself for us

The offering of carnal victims in sacrifice was imposed on our fathers by the holy Trinity itself, the one God of the new and the old testament. These sacrifices were a sign of that most pleasing gift, the sacrifice by which the only God the Son was to offer himself according to the flesh for us in his mercy.

For 'he gave himself up for us as a fragrant offering and a sacrifice to God', according to the teaching of the Apostle. He is true God and true priest, who entered once into the holy of holies for us, taking not the blood of bulls and goats but his own blood. This was foreshadowed in the past by the high priest, who entered the holy of holies each year with blood.

He it is then who showed forth in himself alone all that he knew to be necessary to achieve our redemption—he who at the same time is priest and sacrifice, God and temple: the priest through whom we are reconciled, the sacrifice by which we are reconciled, the temple in which we are reconciled, the God to whom we are reconciled. He alone is priest, sacrifice, and temple, because he is all these as God according to the form of a servant; yet he is not God alone, because he is so along with the Father and the Holy Spirit according to the form of God.

You must hold most firmly then without any shadow of doubt that the only-begotten God, the Word, took flesh and offered himself for us as a fragrant offering and a sacrifice to God. To him with the Father and the Holy Spirit patriarchs, prophets and priests under the old testament offered animals in sacrifice; to him now, under the new testament, with the Father and the Holy Spirit, with whom he is one only God, the holy Catholic Church continually offers the sacrifice of bread and wine in faith and charity throughout the whole world.

For in those carnal victims the flesh and blood of Christ were prefigured, the flesh which he who was without sin was to offer for our sins, the blood which he was to pour out for the forgiveness of our sins. In this sacrifice, however, there is thanksgiving for and commemoration of the flesh of Christ which he has offered for us and of the blood which the same God has poured out for us. Blessed Paul speaks of this in the Acts of the Apostles: 'Take heed to yourselves and to the whole flock, in which the Holy Spirit has placed you as guardians, to rule the Church of God, which he has won by his blood.'

So in the former sacrifices what was to be given to us was intimated in a sign: in this sacrifice, however, what has already been given to us is clearly shown forth.

In those sacrifices the Son of God was foretold, to be put to death for the ungodly; in this sacrifice he is proclaimed now slain for the ungodly. As the Apostle testifies: 'While we were yet helpless, at the right time Christ died for the ungodly', and again 'While we were enemies, we were reconciled to God by the death of his Son.'

RESPONSORY   Col 1:21-22;Rom 3:25
℞ When you were estranged from God, your minds alienated from him by a life of sin, he used Christ's natural body to win you back through his death,* so that he might bring you into his presence holy, pure and blameless.
℣ God offered him so that by his death he should become the means by which men's sins are forgiven, through their faith in him,* so that he might bring you . . .

SATURDAY

℣ The man who lives by the truth comes into the light.
℞ So that his good works may be seen.

THE FIRST READING   Heb 8:1-13
A reading from the letter to the Hebrews

The priesthood of Christ in the New Covenant

The great point of all that we have said is that we have a high priest of exactly this kind. He has his place at the right of the throne of divine Majesty in the heavens, and he is the minister of the sanctuary and of the true Tent of Meeting which the Lord, and not any man, set up. It is the duty of every high priest to offer gifts and sacrifices, and so this one too must have something to offer. In fact, if he were on earth, he would not be a priest at all, since there are others who make the offerings laid down by the Law, and these only maintain the service of a model or a reflection of the heavenly realities. For Moses, when he had the Tent to build, was warned by God who said: 'See that you make everything according to the pattern shown you on the mountain.'

We have seen that he has been given a ministry of a far higher order, and to the same degree it is a better covenant of which he is the mediator, founded on better promises. If that first covenant had been without a fault, there would have been no need for a second one to replace it. And in fact God does find fault with them; he says:

'See, the days are coming—it is the Lord who speaks—
when I will establish a new covenant
with the House of Israel and the House of Judah,
but not a covenant like the one I made with their ancestors
on the day I took them by the hand
to bring them out of the land of Egypt.
They abandoned that covenant of mine,
and so I on my side deserted them. It is the Lord who speaks.
No, this is the covenant I will make
with the House of Israel
when those days arrive—it is the Lord who speaks.
I will put my laws into their minds
and write them on their hearts.
Then I will be their God
and they shall be my people.
There will be no further need for neighbour to try to teach
    neighbour,
or brother to say to brother,
"Learn to know the Lord".

No, they will all know me,
the least no less than the greatest,
since I will forgive their iniquities
and never call their sins to mind.'

By speaking of a new covenant, he implies that the first one is already old. Now anything old only gets more antiquated until in the end it disappears.

RESPONSORY   Heb 8:1,2;9:24

℟ We have a high priest whose place is at the right of the throne of divine Majesty in the heavens,—and he is the minister of the sanctuary and of the true Tent of Meeting,* so that he may appear in the actual presence of God on our behalf.

℣ Christ has entered, not a man-made sanctuary which was only modelled on the real one, but heaven itself,* so that he may appear in the actual presence of God on our behalf.

THE SECOND READING   Or 45,23-4
A reading from the addresses of St Gregory Nazianzen

We shall share in the pasch

We shall share in the pasch, for the present certainly in what is still a figure, though a plainer one than the ancient pasch. (This pasch of the old law was, I venture to say, a more obscure figure, a figure of a figure.) In a short time, however, our sharing will be more perfect and less obscure, when the Word will drink the pasch with us new in the kingdom of his Father, revealing and teaching what he has now shown in a limited way. For what is now being made known is ever new.

What this drink is and what this enjoyment, is for us to learn and for him to teach and to share this teaching with his disciples. For the teaching is food even for the one who feeds others.

Come then, let us also share in the law, not in the letter but in the spirit of the gospel, perfectly and not incompletely, for eternity and not for a period of time only. For our capital let us take not the earthly Jerusalem but our mother city in heaven, not the city now trampled by armies but the one extolled by angels.

Let us not sacrifice young calves or lambs with horns and hoofs, which are for the most part dead, insensate things. But let us offer a sacrifice of praise to God on the altar on high along with the choirs of heaven. Let us go through the first veil, let us come to the second, let us look into the holy of holies.

To say something greater still, let us sacrifice ourselves to God, further, let us go on every day offering ourselves and all our activities. Let us accept everything literally, let us imitate the passion by our sufferings, let us reverence the blood by our blood, let us be eager to climb the cross.

If you are Simon of Cyrene, take up the cross and follow.

If you are crucified with him as a robber, have the honesty to acknowledge God. If he was numbered among the transgressors because of you and your sin, you must become righteous because of him. Adore him who hung upon the cross through your fault; and while he is hanging there, draw some advantage even from your own wickedness; buy salvation by his death, enter paradise with Jesus and learn what is the extent of your deprivation. Contemplate the glories there: let the murmurer die outside with his blasphemy.

If you are Joseph of Arimathea, ask the executioner for the body: make your own the expiation of the world.

If you are Nicodemus, the man who served God by night, prepare him for burial with perfumes.

If you are one or other Mary, or Salome or Joanna, shed tears in the early morning. Be the first to see the stone removed, and perhaps the angels too, and even Jesus himself.

RESPONSORY   Heb 13:12-13;12:4

℟ Jesus suffered outside the gate to sanctify the people with his own blood.* Let us go to him, then, outside the camp, and share his degradation.

℣ In the fight against sin, you have not yet had to keep fighting to the point of death.* Let us go to him, then . . .

HOLY WEEK

PALM SUNDAY OF
THE PASSION OF THE LORD

℣ When I am lifted up from the earth,
℟ I shall draw all things to myself.

THE FIRST READING   Heb 10:1-18
    A reading from the letter to the Hebrews

We are made holy through the offering of Christ

Since the Law has no more than a reflection of these realities,
and no finished picture of them, it is quite incapable of bringing the worshippers to prefection, with the same sacrifices
repeatedly offered year after year. Otherwise, the offering of
them would have stopped, because the worshippers, when they
had been purified once, would have no awareness of sins.
Instead of that, the sins are recalled year after year in the
sacrifices. Bulls' blood and goats' blood are useless for taking
away sins, and this is what he said, on coming into the world:

'You who wanted no sacrifice or oblation,
prepared a body for me.
You took no pleasure in holocausts or sacrifices for sin;
then I said,
just as I was commanded in the scroll of the book,
"God, here I am! I am coming to obey your will." '

Notice that he says first: You did not want what the Law lays
down as the things to be offered, that is: the sacrifices, the
oblations, the holocausts and the sacrifices for sin, and you

took no pleasure in them; and then he says: 'Here I am! I am coming to obey your will.' He is abolishing the first sort to replace it with the second. And this will was for us to be made holy by the offering of his body made once and for all by Jesus Christ.

All the priests stand at their duties every day, offering over and over again the same sacrifices which are quite incapable of taking sins away. He, on the other hand, has offered one single sacrifice for sins, and then taken his place for ever, at the right hand of God, where he is now waiting until his enemies are made into a footstool for him. By virtue of that one single offering, he has achieved the eternal perfection of all whom he is sanctifying. The Holy Spirit assures us of this; for he says, first:

> 'This is the covenant I will make with them
> when those days arrive';

and the Lord then goes on to say:

> 'I will put my laws into their hearts
> and write them on their minds.
> I will never call their sins to mind,
> or their offences.'

When all sins have been forgiven, there can be no more sin offerings.

RESPONSORY   Ps 39:7-8;Heb 10:4

℟ You do not ask for sacrifice and offerings, but you have prepared a body for me. You do not ask for holocaust and victim, then I said:* Here I am, O God, I come to do your will.
℣ The blood of bulls and goats can never take sins away. For this reason, when Christ was about to come into the world, he said: *Here I am, O God . . .

THE SECOND READING Or 9
A reading from the addresses of St Andrew of Crete

Blessed is he who comes in the name of the Lord,
the King of Israel

Come, come, let us go up together to the Mount of Olives. Together let us meet Christ, who is returning today from Bethany and going of his own accord to that holy and blessed passion to complete the mystery of our salvation.

And so he comes, willingly taking the road to Jerusalem, he who came down from the heights for us, to raise us who lie in the depths to exaltation with him, as the revealing word says, 'above all authority and rule and power and above every name that is named'.

He comes without display, without boast. 'He will not contend,' he says, 'or shout out, and no one will hear his voice.' He is gentle and lowly, and his entrance is humble.

Come then, let us run with him as he presses on to his passion. Let us imitate those who have gone out to meet him, not scattering olive branches or garments or palms in his path, but spreading ourselves before him as best we can, with humility of soul and upright purpose. So may we welcome the Word as he comes, so may God who cannot be contained within any bounds, be contained within us.

For he is pleased to have shown us this gentleness, he who is gentle and who 'rides upon the setting sun', which refers to our extreme lowliness. He is pleased to come and live with us and to raise us up or bring us back to him through his kinship with us.

As the first fruits of the whole batch of man he is said to 'ride upon the heaven of heavens to the rising of the sun', which I interpret as his own glory and divinity. But because of his love for man he will not cease until he has raised man's nature from the ground, from one degree of glory to another, and has manifested it with himself on high.

So it is ourselves that we must spread under Christ's feet, not coats or lifeless branches or shoots of trees, matter which wastes away and delights the eye only for a few brief hours. But we have clothed ourselves with Christ's grace, or with the whole Christ—'for as many of you as were baptized into Christ have put on Christ'—so let us spread ourselves like coats under his feet.

As those who were formerly scarlet from sin but became white as wool through the purification of saving baptism, let us offer not palm branches but the prizes of victory to the conqueror of death.

Today let us too give voice with the children to that sacred chant, as we wave the spiritual branches of our soul: 'Blessed is he who comes in the name of the Lord, the King of Israel.'

RESPCNSORY   Jn 12:12,13;Mt 21:8,9
R̷ When the people heard that Jesus was on his way to Jerusalem, they went out to meet him. Great crowds of people spread their cloaks on the road while others spread branches in his path, and they shouted,* Hosanna to the Son of David! Blessings on him who comes in the name of the Lord!
V̷ The crowds who went in front of him and those who followed all shouted aloud,* Hosanna to the Son of David! . . .

MONDAY

℣ When I am lifted up from the earth,
℟ I shall draw all things to myself.

THE FIRST READING   Heb 10:19-39
            A reading from the letter to the Hebrews

Perseverance in faith. Awaiting the judgment of God

Through the blood of Jesus we have the right to enter the
sanctuary, by a new way which he has opened for us, a living
opening through the curtain, that is to say, his body. And we
have the supreme high priest over all the house of God. So as
we go in, let us be sincere in heart and filled with faith, our
minds sprinkled and free from any trace of bad conscience and
our bodies washed with pure water. Let us keep firm in the
hope we profess, because the one who made the promise is
faithful. Let us be concerned for each other, to stir a response
in love and good works. Do not stay away from the meetings
of the community, as some do, but encourage each other to go;
the more so as you see the Day drawing near.

   If, after we have been given knowledge of the truth, we
should deliberately commit any sins, then there is no longer
any sacrifice for them. There will be left only the dreadful
prospect of judgment and of the raging fire that is to burn
rebels. Anyone who disregards the Law of Moses is ruthlessly
put to death on the word of two witnesses or three; and you
may be sure that anyone who tramples on the Son of God, and
who treats the blood of the covenant which sanctified him as
if it were not holy, and who insults the Spirit of grace, will be
condemned to a far severer punishment. We are all aware who
it was that said: 'Vengeance is mine; I will repay.' And again:

'The Lord will judge his people.' It is a dreadful thing to fall into the hands of the living God.

Remember all the sufferings that you had to meet after you received the light, in earlier days; sometimes by being yourselves publicly exposed to insults and violence, and sometimes as associates of others who were treated in the same way. For you not only shared in the sufferings of those who were in prison, but you happily accepted being stripped of your belongings, knowing that you owned something that was better and lasting. Be as confident now, then, since the reward is so great. You will need endurance to do God's will and gain what he has promised.

Only a little while now, a very little while,
and the one that is coming will have come; he will not delay.
The righteous man will live by faith,
but if he draws back, my soul will take no pleasure in him.

You and I are not the sort of people who draw back, and are lost by it; we are the sort who keep faithful until our souls are saved.

RESPONSORY   Heb 10:35,36;Lk 21:19
℟ Do not lose courage.* You will need endurance to do God's will and gain what he has promised.
℣ Your endurance will win you your lives.* You will need endurance . . .

THE SECOND READING   Sermon Guelf 3
    A reading from the sermons of St Augustine

Let us also boast in the cross of the Lord

The passion of our Lord and Saviour Jesus Christ gives us the confidence of glory and a lesson in the endurance of suffering.

Is there anything which the hearts of the faithful may not

promise themselves from the grace of God? It was not enough that the only Son of God, co-eternal with the Father, should be born as man from man for them—he even died for them at the hands of men, whom he had created.

What God promises us for the future is great, but what we recall as already done for us is much greater. When Christ died for the wicked, where were they or what were they? Who can doubt that he will give the saints his life, since he has already given them his death? Why is human weakness slow to believe that men will one day live with God?

A much more incredible thing has already happened: God died for men.

For who is Christ, unless that which 'in the beginning was the Word, and the Word was with God, and the Word was God'? This Word of God 'became flesh and dwelt among us': for in himself he was incapable of dying for us, unless he had assumed mortal flesh from us. In this way the immortal one was able to die, in this way he wished to give life to mortals; he would later make them sharers in himself, since he had first shared in what was theirs. For of ourselves we did not have the ability to live, as of himself he did not have the ability to die.

Accordingly he carried out a wonderful transaction with us through our mutual sharing: he died from what was ours, we will live from what is his.

So far from being ashamed at the death of the Lord our God, we must have the fullest trust in it; it must be our greatest boast, for by assuming from us death, which he found in us, he pledged most faithfully to give us life in himself, which we could not have of ourselves.

He loved us so much that what we deserved by sin he who was without sin suffered for sinners. Surely then he who justifies will give us what justice gives. Surely he whose promise is truthful will give us the rewards of the saints, since though without wickedness himself he bore the punishment of the wicked.

So, brethren, let us acknowledge without fear or indeed let

us declare publicly that Christ was crucified for us. Let us announce it not trembling but rejoicing, not with shame but boasting.

The apostle Paul saw him, and approved a cause for boasting. Though he had many great things, divine things, to recall about Christ, he did not say that he boasted of Christ's marvels, that Christ created the world when he was God with the Father and ruled the world when he was man as we were; but what he did say was 'Far be it from me to glory except in the cross of our Lord Jesus Christ.'

RESPONSORY

℞ Lord, we venerate your cross as we recall your blessed passion.* You who suffered for our sake, have compassion on us.

℣ Come to the help of your servants whom you redeemed with your precious blood.* You have suffered for our sake . . .

TUESDAY

℣ When I am lifted up from the earth,
℞ I shall draw all things to myself.

THE FIRST READING   Heb 12:1-13
  A reading from the letter to the Hebrews

With Christ as our leader, we go forward to the struggle

Therefore, since we are surrounded by so great a cloud of witnesses, let us also lay aside every weight, and sin which clings so closely, and let us run with perseverance the race that is set before us, looking to Jesus the pioneer and perfecter of our faith, who for the joy that was set before him endured the cross, despising the shame, and is seated at the right hand of the throne of God.

Consider him who endured from sinners such hostility against himself, so that you may not grow weary or faint-hearted. In your struggle against sin you have not yet resisted to the point of shedding your blood. And have you forgotten the exhortation which addresses you as sons?

'My son, do not regard lightly the discipline of the Lord, nor lose courage when you are punished by him, For the Lord disciplines him whom he loves, and chastises every son whom he receives.'

It is for discipline that you have to endure. God is treating you as sons; for what son is there whom his father does not discipline? If you are left without discipline, in which all have participated, then you are illegitimate children and not sons. Besides this, we have had earthly fathers to discipline us and we respected them. Shall we not much more be subject to the Father of spirits and live? For they disciplined us for a short time at their pleasure, but he disciplines us for our good, that we may share his holiness. For the moment all discipline seems painful rather than pleasant; later it yields the peaceful fruit of righteousness to those who have been trained by it.

Therefore lift your drooping hands and strengthen your weak knees, and make straight paths for your feet, so that what is lame may not be put out of joint but rather be healed.

RESPONSORY   Heb 12:2;Phil 2:8
℟ Jesus, who leads us in our faith and brings it to perfection, for the sake of the joy which was still in the future, endured the cross,* and now he has taken his place at God's right hand.
℣ He was humble and walked the path of obedience to death,* and now he has taken his place at God's right hand.

THE SECOND READING   Chs 15,35
A reading from the book of St Basil *On the Holy Spirit*

There is one death for the world, and one resurrection
from the dead

The providence of our God and Saviour in regard to man consists of his recall from the fall and his return to close communion with God from the estrangement caused by his disobedience. This was the purpose of Christ's dwelling in the flesh, the pattern of his life described in the gospels, his sufferings, the cross, the burial, the resurrection; so that man could be saved, and could recover, through imitating Christ, the adoption of former times.

So, for perfection of life it is necessary not only to imitate Christ, in the examples of gentleness, and humility, and patience which he gave us in his life, but also to imitate him in his death, as Paul the imitator of Christ says: 'Becoming like him in his death, that if possible I may attain the resurrection from the dead.'

How then do we become like him in his death? By having been buried with him through baptism. But how does this burial take place? What benefit has this imitation? First of all one must break with one's life of the past. This is impossible, unless one is born again, as the Lord said. For regeneration, as is evident from the word itself, is the beginning of a second life. Consequently, before beginning this second life, we must bring the first to an end. As in the double course (where the competitors must run to the turning point and back to the start again) a halt, a brief respite separates the outward run and the return, so also for a change of life it seemed necessary that death intervene between the two lives, to make an end of all that went before and a beginning of all that follows.

How do we accomplish the descent into hell? By imitating through baptism the burial of Christ. For the bodies of the baptized are buried as it were in the water. Baptism then indicates symbolically the laying aside of the works of the flesh, as the Apostle says: 'You were circumcised with a circumcision made without hands, by putting off the body of flesh, in the circumcision of Christ, having been buried with him in baptism.' Baptism, as it were, cleanses the soul of the pollution which comes from the mind set on the flesh, as it is written 'You will wash me, and I shall be whiter than snow.' Consequently, we know only one baptism which saves, since there is one death on behalf of the world and one resurrection from the dead, and baptism is the figure of these.

RESPONSORY   Rom 6:3,5,4

℟ When we were baptized in Christ Jesus we were baptized in his death;* if in union with him we have imitated his death, we shall also imitate him in his resurrection.

℣ When we were baptized we went into the tomb with him and joined him in death;* if in union with him . . .

WEDNESDAY

℣ When I am lifted up from the earth,
℟ I shall draw all things to myself.

THE FIRST READING   Heb 12:14-29
A reading from the letter to the Hebrews

We have come to the mountain of the living God

Always be wanting peace with all people, and the holiness without which no one can ever see the Lord. Be careful that no one is deprived of the grace of God and that no root of bitterness should begin to grow and make trouble; this can poison a whole community. And be careful that there is no immorality, or that any of you does not degrade religion like Esau, who sold his birthright for one single meal. As you know, when he wanted to obtain the blessing afterwards, he was rejected and, though he pleaded for it with tears, he was unable to elicit a change of heart.

What you have come to is nothing known to the senses: not a blazing fire, or a gloom turning to total darkness, or a storm; or trumpeting thunder or the great voice speaking which made everyone that heard it beg that no more should be said to them. They were appalled at the order that was given: 'If even an animal touches the mountain, it must be stoned.' The whole scene was so terrible that Moses said: 'I am afraid,' and was trembling with fright. But what you have come to is Mount Zion and the city of the living God, the heavenly Jerusalem where the millions of angels have gathered for the festival, with the whole Church in which everyone is a 'first-born son' and a citizen of heaven. You have come to God himself, the supreme Judge, and been placed with spirits of the saints who have been made perfect; and to Jesus, the mediator who brings a new covenant and a blood for purification which pleads more insistently than Abel's. Make sure that you never refuse to listen when he speaks. The people who refused to listen to the warning from a voice on earth could not escape their punishment, and how shall we escape if we turn away from a voice that warns us from heaven? That time his voice made the earth shake, but now he has given us this promise: 'I will make the earth shake once more and not only the earth but heaven as well.' The words 'once more' show that since the things being shaken are created things, they are going to be changed, so that the unshakeable things will be left. We have been given possession of an unshakeable kingdom. Let us therefore hold on to the grace that we have been given and use it to worship God in the way that he finds acceptable, in reverence and fear. For our God is a consuming fire.

RESPONSORY   Cf Deut 5:23,24;cf Heb 12:22
When you heard the voice coming out of the darkness, while
the mountain of Sinai was all on fire, you came to Moses and
said,* See, how the Lord our God has shown us his glory and
his greatness.

℣ Now you have come to mount Sion and the city of the living
God, the heavenly Jerusalem.* See, how the Lord our
God . . .

THE SECOND READING   Tr 84,1-2
A reading from the homilies of St Augustine on
St John's Gospel

The fulness of love

Dearly beloved, that fulness of love with which we must love
one another, the Lord defined when he said, 'Greater love has
no man than this, that a man lay down his life for his friends.'
There follows from this what the same evangelist John says
in his epistle: 'As Christ laid down his life for us, so ought we
lay down our lives for the brethren', loving one another as he
loved us, he who laid down his life for us.

Doubtless this is what one reads in the Proverbs of Solomon:
'If you sit down to eat at a ruler's table, observe carefully
what is before you; and know that you must prepare a similar
meal.' For what is the ruler's table, if not where there is taken
the body and blood of him who laid down his life for us? And
what is 'to sit at it', if not to approach humbly? What is 'to
observe carefully what is before you', if not to ponder worthily
so great a favour? What does it mean 'know that you must prepare a similar meal', if not what I have said already, that as
Christ laid down his life for us, so we too ought to lay down
our lives for our brethren. In the words of the apostle Peter:
'Christ suffered for us, leaving us an example, that we should
follow in his steps.' This is 'to prepare a similar meal'. This

the blessed martyrs did with burning love. If our celebration of their memory is not an empty one, and if we approach the Lord's table in the banquet in which they too ate and had their fill, then as they prepared such a meal, so should we also.

So in fact at this table we do not commemorate them in the same way as we commemorate others who rest in peace, in order to pray for them also. We commemorate them rather so that they may pray for us, that we may follow closely in their footsteps; for they have reached the fulness of that love than which the Lord said there could be none greater. What they showed to their brothers was such as they equally received from the Lord's table.

This must not be taken to mean that we can be the equals of the Lord Christ because we have carried our witness for him to the shedding of blood. He had the power to lay down his life, and to take it again; we, on the other hand, do not live as long as we want to live, and we die even if we do not want to die. He, by dying, at once destroyed death in himself, we are freed from death in his death. His flesh did not see corruption, while ours, after corruption, will put on incorruption through him at the end of time. He had no need of us in order to save us, but we can do nothing without him. He gave himself as the vine to us the branches and we cannot have life apart from him.

Finally, even if brothers die for brothers, still no martyr's blood is shed for the forgiveness of the brothers' sins—this is what Christ did for us. In this he did not give us something to imitate, but something for thanksgiving. In so far as the martyrs, then, shed their blood for their brothers, what they showed was such as they received from the Lord's table. So let us love one another as Christ loved us and gave himself for us.

RESPONSORY   1 Jn 4:9,11,10

℟ God's love for us was revealed when he sent into the world his only Son so that we could have life through him.* Since God loved us so much, we too should love one another.

℣ God first loved us and sent his Son to be the sacrifice that takes our sins away.* Since God loved us so much . . .

HOLY THURDSAY

℣ When I am lifted up from the earth,
℟ I shall draw all things to myself.

THE FIRST READING   Heb 4:14-5:10
A reading from the letter to the Hebrews

Jesus Christ, our high priest

Since in Jesus, the Son of God, we have the supreme high priest who has gone through to the highest heaven, we must never let go of the faith that we have professed. For it is not as if we had a high priest who was incapable of feeling our weaknesses with us; but we have one who has been tempted in every way that we are, though he is without sin. Let us be confident, then, in approaching the throne of grace, that we shall have mercy from him and find grace when we are in need of help.

Every high priest has been taken out of mankind and is appointed to act for men in their relations with God, to offer gifts and sacrifices for sins; and so he can sympathize with those who are ignorant or uncertain because he too lives in the limitations of weakness. That is why he has to make sin offerings for himself as well as for the people. No one takes this honour on himself, but each one is called by God, as Aaron was. Nor did Christ give himself the glory of becoming high priest, but he had it from the one who said to him: 'You are my son, today I have become your father,' and in another text: 'You are a priest of the order of Melchizedek, and for ever.' During his life on earth, he offered up prayer and entreaty, aloud and in silent tears, to the one who had the power to save him out of death, and he submitted so humbly that his prayer was heard. Although he was Son, he learnt to obey through suffering; but having been made perfect, he became for all who obey him the source of eternal salvation and was acclaimed by God with the title of high priest of the order of Melchizedek.

RESPONSORY   Heb 5:8,9,7
℞ Although he was the Son of God, Christ learnt to obey through suffering,* and he became for all who obey him the source of eternal salvation.
℣ During his life on earth, he offered up prayer aloud, and he submitted so humbly that his prayer was heard,* and he became for all who obey him . . .

THE SECOND READING   Nn 65-71
A reading from the homily of Melito of Sardis
on the Pasch

The Lamb slain in sacrifice rescued us from death to life

The prophets announced many wonderful things about the Passover mystery which is Christ. To him be glory forever. Amen.

He descended from heaven to earth for the sake of suffering mankind, clothed himself with a human nature through the Virgin Mary, and appearing in our midst as a man with a body capable of suffering, took upon himself the suffering of those who suffered. By his Spirit which could not die, he slew death, the slayer of men. Led forth like a lamb, slain like a sheep, he ransomed us from the servitude of the world, just as he ransomed Israel from the land of Egypt. He freed us from the slavery of the devil, just as he had freed Israel from the hand of Pharaoh; and he has marked our souls with the signs of his own blood. He has clothed death with dishonour and he has grieved the devil, just as Moses dishonoured and grieved Pharaoh. He has punished wickedness and taken away the children of injustice, just as Moses punished Egypt and un-childed it. He has brought us from slavery to freedom, from darkness to light, from death to life, from tyranny to an eternal kingdom.

He is the Passover of our salvation. He was present in many so as to endure many things. In Abel he was slain; in Isaac bound; in Jacob a stranger; in Joseph sold; in Moses exposed; in David persecuted; in the prophets dishonoured. He became incarnate of the Virgin. Not a bone of his was broken on the tree. He was buried in the earth, but he rose from the dead, and was lifted up to the heights of heaven. He is the silent lamb, the slain lamb, who was born of Mary the fair ewe. He was seized from the flock and dragged away to slaughter. Towards evening he was sacrificed, and at night he was buried. But he who had no bone broken upon the cross, was not corrupted in the earth, for he rose from the dead and raised up man from the depths of the grave.

RESPONSORY   Rom 3:23-25;Jn 1:29

℞ All men have sinned and are far away from God's saving presence, but by the free gift of God's grace they are all redeemed through Christ Jesus, who sets them free.* God offered him so that by his death he should become the means by which men's sins are forgiven, through their faith in him. ℣ Look, there is the Lamb of God; it is he who takes away the sin of the world.* God offered him . . .

GOOD FRIDAY

℣ False witnesses rise against me,
℟ And falsehood has deceived itself.

THE FIRST READING   Heb 9:11-28
A reading from the letter to the Hebrews

*Christ, the high priest, through the shedding of his own blood
has entered the sanctuary once and for all*

Now Christ has come, as the high priest of all the blessings
which were to come. He has passed through the greater, the
more perfect tent, which is better than the one made by men's
hands because it is not of this created order; and he has
entered the sanctuary once and for all, taking with him not the
blood of goats and bull calves, but his own blood, having won
an eternal redemption for us. The blood of goats and bulls and
the ashes of a heifer are sprinkled on those who have incurred
defilement and they restore the holiness of their outward lives;
how much more effectively the blood of Christ, who offered
himself as the perfect sacrifice to God through the eternal
Spirit, can purify our inner self from dead actions so that we
do our service to the living God.

He brings a new covenant, as the mediator, only so that the
people who were called to an eternal inheritance may actually
receive what was promised: his death took place to cancel the
sins that infringed the earlier covenant. Now wherever a will
is in question, the death of the testator must be established;
indeed, it only becomes valid with that death, since it is not
meant to have any effect while the testator is still alive. That
explains why even the earlier covenant needed something to
be killed in order to take effect, and why, after Moses had an-

nounced all the commandments of the Law to the people, he took the calves' blood, the goats' blood and some water, and with these he sprinkled the book itself and all the people, using scarlet wool and hyssop; saying as he did so: 'This is the blood of the covenant that God has laid down for you.' After that, he sprinkled the tent and all the liturgical vessels with blood in the same way. In fact, according to the Law almost everything has to be purified with blood; and if there is no shedding of blood, there is no remission. Obviously, only the copies of heavenly things can be purified in this way, and the heavenly things themselves have to be purified by a higher sort of sacrifice than this. It is not as though Christ had entered a man-made sanctuary which was only modelled on the real one; but it was heaven itself, so that he could appear in the actual presence of God on our behalf. And he does not have to offer himself again and again, like the high priest going into the sanctuary year after year with the blood that is not his own, or else he would have had to suffer over and over again since the world began. Instead of that, he has made his appearance once and for all, now at the end of the last age, to do away with sin by sacrificing himself. Since men only die once, and after that comes judgment, so Christ, too, offers himself only once to take the faults of many on himself, and when he appears a second time, it will not be to deal with sin but to reward with salvation those who are waiting for him.

RESPONSORY   Cf Is 53:7,12
℟ He was led out as a lamb that is led to the slaughterhouse; harshly dealt with, he never opened his mouth; he was given over to death,* so as to give life to his people.
℣ He surrendered himself to death and was ranked with sinners,* so as to give life to his people.

THE SECOND READING   Cat 3:13–19
A reading from the instructions of St John Chrysostom
to catechumens

The power of the blood of Christ

Do you wish to know of the power of Christ's blood? Let us
go back to the ancient accounts of what took place in Egypt,
where Christ's blood is foreshadowed.

Moses said: 'Sacrifice a lamb without blemish and smear
the doors with its blood.' What does this mean? Can the blood
of a sheep without reason save man who is endowed with
reason? Yes, Moses replies, not because it is blood but
because it is a figure of the Lord's blood. So today if the devil
sees, not the blood of the figure smeared on the doorposts, but
the blood of the reality smeared on the lips of the faithful,
which are the doors of the temple of Christ, with all the more
reason will he draw back.

Do you wish to learn from another source the power of
this blood? See where it began to flow, from what spring it
flowed down from the cross, from the Master's side. The
gospel relates that when Christ had died and was still hanging
on the cross, the soldier approached him and pierced his side
with the spear, and at once there came out water and blood.
The one was a symbol of baptism, the other of the mysteries.
That soldier, then, pierced his side: he breached the wall of
the holy temple, and I found the treasure and acquired the
wealth. Similarly with the lamb. The Jews slaughtered it in
sacrifice, and I gathered the fruit of that sacrifice—salvation.

'There came out from his side water and blood.' Dearly
beloved, do not pass the secret of this great mystery by without
reflection. For I have another secret mystical interpretation to
give. I said that baptism and the mysteries were symbolized
in that blood and water. It is from these two that the holy
Church has been born 'by the washing of regeneration and the
renewal of the Holy Spirit', by baptism and by the mysteries.

Now the symbols of baptism and the mysteries came from his side. It was from his side, then, that Christ formed the Church, as from the side of Adam he formed Eve.

That is why in his account of the first man Moses has the words, 'bone of my bone and flesh of my flesh,' giving us a hint here of the Master's side. For as at that time God took a rib from Adam's side and formed woman, so Christ gave us blood and water from his side and formed the Church. Just as then he took the rib while Adam was in a deep sleep, so now he gave the blood and water after his death.

Have you seen how Christ has united his bride to himself? Have you seen with what kind of food he feeds us all? By the same food we are formed and are fed. As a woman feeds her child with her own blood and milk, so too Christ himself continually feeds those whom he has begotten with his own blood.

RESPONSORY   1 Pet 1:18-19;Eph 2:18;1 Jn 1:7
℟ Your ransom was not paid in anything corruptible, neither in silver nor gold, but in the precious blood of Christ, a lamb without blemish.* Through him we all have access to the Father in the one Spirit.
℣ The blood of Jesus Christ, the Son of God, purifies us from all sin.* Through him we all have access . . .

HOLY SATURDAY

℣ Uphold my cause and defend me.
℟ By your promise give me life.

THE FIRST READING   Heb 4:1-13
            A reading from the letter to the Hebrews

We must do everything we can to reach God's place of rest

Be careful: the promise of reaching the place of rest he had
for them still holds good, and none of you must think that he
has come too late for it. We received the Good News exactly
as they did; but hearing the message did them no good
because they did not share the faith of those who listened. We,
however, who have faith, shall reach a place of rest, as in the
text: 'And so, in anger, I swore that not one would reach the
place of rest I had for them.' God's work was undoubtedly all
finished at the beginning of the world; as one text says, re-
ferring to the seventh day: 'After all his work God rested on
the seventh day.' The text we are considering says: 'They
shall not reach the place of rest I had for them.' It is established, then, that there would be some people who would reach
it, and since those who first heard the Good News failed to
reach it through their disobedience, God fixed another day
when, much later, he said 'today' through David in the text
already quoted: 'If only you would listen to him today; do not
harden your hearts.' If Joshua had led them into this place of
rest, God would not later on have spoken so much of another
day. There must still be, therefore, a place of rest reserved for
God's people, the seventh-day rest, since to reach the place of
rest is to rest after your work, as God did after his. We must
therefore do everything we can to reach this place of rest, or

some of you might copy this example of disobedience and be lost.

The word of God is something alive and active: it cuts like any double-edged sword but more finely: it can slip through the place where the soul is divided from the spirit, or joints from the marrow; it can judge the secret emotions and thoughts. No created thing can hide from him; everything is uncovered and open to the eyes of the one to whom we must give account of ourselves.

RESPONSORY   Cf Mt 27:66,60,62

℞ They buried the Lord, made the tomb secure and rolled a stone across the entrance,* and they placed soldiers there to guard the body.

℣ The chief priests went to Pilate and asked for a guard,* and they placed soldiers there to guard the body.

THE SECOND READING

A reading from an ancient homily for Holy Saturday

The Lord's descent into hell

What is happening? Today there is a great silence over the earth, a great silence, and stillness, a great silence because the King sleeps; the earth was in terror and was still, because God slept in the flesh and raised up those who were sleeping from the ages. God has died in the flesh, and the underworld has trembled.

Truly he goes to seek out our first parent like a lost sheep; he wishes to visit those who sit in darkness and in the shadow of death. He goes to free the prisoner Adam and his fellow-prisoner Eve from their pains, he who is God, and Adam's son.

The Lord goes in to them holding his victorious weapon, his cross. When Adam, the first created man, sees him, he strikes his breast in terror and calls out to all: 'My Lord be with you all.' And Christ in reply says to Adam: 'And with your spirit.' And grasping his hand he raises him up, saying: 'Awake, O sleeper, and arise from the dead, and Christ shall give you light.

'I am your God, who for your sake became your son, who for you and your descendants now speak and command with authority those in prison: Come forth, and those in darkness: Have light, and those who sleep: Rise.

'I command you: Awake, sleeper, I have not made you to be held a prisoner in the underworld. Arise from the dead; I am the life of the dead. Arise, O man, work of my hands, arise, you who were fashioned in my image. Rise, let us go hence; for you in me and I in you, together we are one undivided person.

'For you, I your God became your son; for you, I the Master took on your form, that of slave; for you, I who am above the heavens came on earth and under the earth; for you, man, I became as a man without help, free among the dead; for you, who left a garden, I was handed over to Jews from a garden and crucified in a garden.

'Look at the spittle on my face, which I received because of you, in order to restore you to that first divine inbreathing at creation. See the blows on my cheeks, which I accepted in order to refashion your distorted form to my own image.

'See the scourging of my back, which I accepted in order to disperse the load of your sins which was laid upon your back. See my hands nailed to the tree for a good purpose, for you, who stretched out your hand to the tree for an evil one.

'I slept on the cross and a sword pierced my side, for you, who slept in paradise and brought forth Eve from your side. My side healed the pain of your side; my sleep will release you from your sleep in Hades; my sword has checked the sword which was turned against you.

'But arise, let us go hence. The enemy brought you out of the land of paradise; I will reinstate you, no longer in paradise, but on the throne of heaven. I denied you the tree of life, which was a figure, but now I myself am united to you, I who am life. I posted the cherubim to guard you as they would slaves; now I make the cherubim worship you as they would God.

'The cherubim throne has been prepared, the bearers are ready and waiting, the bridal chamber is in order, the food is provided, the everlasting houses and rooms are in readiness, the treasures of good things have been opened; the kingdom of heaven has been prepared before the ages.'

RESPONSORY

R̥. Our shepherd, the source of living water, has departed. At his passing the sun was darkened, for he who held the first man captive is now taken captive himself.* Today our Saviour has shattered the bars and burst the gates of death.

V̥ He has torn down the barricade of hell and overthrown the power of Satan.* Today our Saviour . . .

EASTER SUNDAY
Eastertide begins

THE FIRST READING   Ex 14:15-15:1
A reading from the book of Exodus

The people of Israel walked on dry ground through the sea

The Lord said to Moses, 'Why do you cry to me? Tell the people of Israel to go forward. Lift up your rod, and stretch out your hand over the sea and divide it, that the people of Israel may go on dry ground through the sea. And I will harden the hearts of the Egyptians so that they shall go in after them, and I will get glory over Pharaoh and all his host, his chariots, and his horsemen. And the Egyptians shall know that I am the Lord, when I have gotten glory over Pharaoh, his chariots, and his horsemen.'

Then the angel of God who went before the host of Israel moved and went behind them; and the pillar of cloud moved from before them and stood behind them, coming between the host of Egypt and the host of Israel. And there was the cloud and the darkness; and the night passed without one coming near the other all night.

Then Moses stretched out his hand over the sea; and the Lord drove the sea back by a strong east wind all night, and made the sea dry land, and the waters were divided. And the people of Israel went into the midst of the sea on dry ground, the waters being a wall to them on their right hand and on their left. The Egyptians pursued, and went in after them into the midst of the sea, all Pharaoh's horses, his chariots, and his horsemen. And in the morning watch the Lord in the pillar of fire and of cloud looked down upon the host of the Egyptians, and discomfited the host of the Egyptians, clogging their chariot wheels so that they drove heavily; and the Egyptians said, 'Let us flee from before Israel: for the Lord fights for them against the Egyptians.'

Then the Lord said to Moses, 'Stretch out your hand over the sea, that the water may come back upon the Egyptians, upon their chariots, and upon their horsemen.' So Moses stretched forth his hand over the sea, and the sea returned to its wonted flow when the morning appeared; and the Egyptians fled into it, and the Lord routed the Egyptians in the midst of the sea. The waters returned and covered the chariots and the horsemen and all the host of Pharaoh that had followed them into the sea; not so much as one of them remained. But the people of Israel walked on dry ground through the sea, the waters being a wall to them on their right hand and on their left.

Thus the Lord saved Israel that day from the hand of the Egyptians; and Israel saw the Egyptians dead upon the sea-shore. And Israel saw the great work which the Lord did against the Egyptians, and the people feared the Lord; and they believed in the Lord and in his servant Moses.

Then Moses and the people of Israel sang this song to the Lord, saying:

Antiphon: Let us sing to the Lord: glorious is his triumph.

Canticle: Ex 15:1-6,17-18

I will sing to the Lord, glorious his triumph!
Horse and rider he has thrown into the sea!

The Lord is my strength, my song, my salvation.
This is my God and I extol him,
my father's God and I give him praise.
The Lord is a warrior! The Lord is his name.

The chariots of Pharaoh he hurled into the sea,
the flower of his army is drowned in the sea.

The deeps hide them; they sank like a stone.
Your right hand, Lord, glorious in its power,
your right hand, Lord, has shattered the enemy.

You will lead them and plant them on your mountain,
the place, O Lord, where you have made your home,
the sanctuary, Lord, which your hands have made.
The Lord will reign for ever and ever!

Antiphon: Let us sing to the Lord: glorious is his triumph.

PRAYER
Lord God,
you have revealed, in the light of the New Testament,
the meaning of the miracles you did in former days.
The Red Sea was to be a symbol of holy baptism,
and the race set free from captivity
was to prefigure the sacraments of the Christian people.
Let all the nations who, by their faith,
have succeeded to Israel's privilege,
be regenerated by sharing in your Spirit.
Through Christ our Lord.

May the peoples of the world become true sons of Abraham
and prove worthy of the heritage of Israel.
(We ask this) through Christ our Lord.

THE SECOND READING   Ezek 36:16-28
        A reading from the prophet Ezekiel

I shall pour clean water over you, I shall give you a new heart

The word of the Lord was addressed to me as follows: 'Son of
man, the members of the House of Israel used to live in their
own land, but they defiled it by their conduct and actions. I
then discharged my fury at them because of the blood they
shed in their land and the idols with which they defiled it. I
scattered them among the nations and dispersed them in

foreign countries. I sentenced them as their conduct and actions deserved. And now they have profaned my holy name among the nations where they have gone, so that people say of them. "These are the people of the Lord; they have been exiled from his land." But I have been concerned about my holy name, which the House of Israel has profaned among the nations where they have gone. And so, say to the House of Israel, "The Lord says this: I am not doing this for your sake, House of Israel, but for the sake of my holy name, which you have profaned among the nations where you have gone. I mean to display the holiness of my great name, which has been profaned among the nations, which you have profaned among them. And the nations will learn that I am the Lord—it is the Lord who speaks—when I display my holiness for your sake before their eyes. Then I am going to take you from among the nations and gather you together from all the foreign countries, and bring you home to your own land. I shall pour clean water over you and you will be cleansed; I shall cleanse you of all your defilement and all your idols. I shall give you a new heart, and put a new spirit in you; I shall remove the heart of stone from your bodies and give you a heart of flesh instead. I shall put my spirit in you, and make you keep my laws and sincerely respect my observances. You will live in the land which I gave your ancestors. You shall be my people and I will be your God." '

Antiphon: Like the deer that yearns for running streams, so my soul is yearning for you, my God.

Psalms 41(42):2-3,5;42(43):3-4

Like the deer that yearns
for running streams,
so my soul is yearning
for you, my God.

My soul is thirsting for God,
the God of my life;

when can I enter and see
the face of God?

These things will I remember
as I pour out my soul:
how I would lead the rejoicing crowd
into the house of God,
amid cries of gladness and thanksgiving,
the throng wild with joy.

O send forth your light and your truth;
let these be my guide.
Let them bring me to your holy mountain
to the place where you dwell.

And I will come to the altar of God,
the God of my joy.
My redeemer, I will thank you on the harp,
O God, my God.

Antiphon: Like the deer that yearns for running streams, so my
soul is yearning for you, my God.

PRAYER
Lord God, look down with favour
from your eternal light and unchangeable power
on the sacrament of the whole Church.
Carry out the work of man's salvation
in the tranquillity of your eternal plan.
Let the whole world experience and see
what had been deprived of hope, raised up,
what had grown old, renewed,
and all things made whole
by him who first created them, Jesus Christ, your Son,
our Lord, who lives and reigns for ever and ever.

THE THIRD READING   Rom 6:3-11
A reading from the letter of St Paul to the Romans

Christ being raised from the dead will never die again

Do you not know that all of us who have been baptized into
Christ Jesus were baptized into his death? We were buried
therefore with him by baptism into death, so that as Christ
was raised from the dead by the glory of the Father, we too
might walk in newness of life.

For if we have been united with him in a death like his,
we shall certainly be united with him in a resurrection like his.
We know that our old self was crucified with him so that the
sinful body might be destroyed, and we might no longer be
enslaved to sin. For he who has died is freed from sin. But if
we have died with Christ, we believe that we shall also live
with him. For we know that Christ being raised from the dead
will never die again; death no longer has dominion over him.
The death he died he died to sin, once for all, but the life he
lives he lives to God. So you also must consider yourselves
dead to sin and alive to God in Christ Jesus.

Antiphon: Alleluia, alleluia, alleluia.

Ps 117(118):1-2,15c-17,22-23

Give thanks to the Lord for he is good,
for his love endures for ever.
Let the sons of Israel say:
His love endures for ever.

The Lord's right hand has triumphed;
his right hand raised me.
I shall not die, I shall live
and recount his deeds.

The stone which the builders rejected
has become the corner stone.

This is the work of the Lord,
a marvel in our eyes.

Antiphon: Alleluia, alleluia, alleluia.

THE FOURTH READING   Mt 28:1-10
A reading from the holy Gospel according
to Matthew

*He has risen from the dead and he is going
before you to Galilee*

After the sabbath, toward the dawn of the first day of the
week, Mary Magdalene and the other Mary went to see the
sepulchre. And behold, there was a great earthquake; for an
angel of the Lord descended from heaven and came and rolled
back the stone, and sat upon it. His appearance was like
lightning, and his raiment white as snow. And for fear of him
the guards trembled and became like dead men. But the angel
said to the women, 'Do not be afraid; for I know that you seek
Jesus who was crucified. He is not here; for he has risen, as he
said. Come, see the place where he lay. Then go quickly and
tell his disciples that he has risen from the dead, and behold,
he is going before you to Galilee; there you will see him. Lo, I
have told you.' So they departed quickly from the tomb with
fear and great joy, and ran to tell his disciples. And behold,
Jesus met them and said, 'Hail!' And they came up and took
hold of his feet and worshipped him. Then Jesus said to them,
'Do not be afraid; go and tell my brethren to go to Galilee,
and there they will see me.'

TE DEUM

We praise you, O God:
we acclaim you as the Lord.

Everlasting Father,
all the world bows down before you.

All the angels sing your praise,
the hosts of heaven and all the angelic powers,

    all the cherubim and seraphim
    call out to you in unending song:

        Holy, Holy, Holy,
        is the Lord God of angel hosts!

The heavens and the earth are filled
with your majesty and glory.

    The glorious band of apostles,
    the noble company of prophets,

the white-robed army who shed their blood for Christ,
all sing your praise.

    And to the ends of the earth
    your holy Church proclaims her faith in you:

        Father, whose majesty is boundless,
        your true and only Son, who is to be adored,
        the Holy Spirit sent to be our Advocate.

You, Christ, are the king of glory,
Son of the eternal Father.

    When you took our nature to save mankind
    you did not shrink from birth in the Virgin's womb.

You overcame the power of death
opening the Father's kingdom to all who believe in you.

    Enthroned at God's right hand in the glory of the Father,
    you will come in judgment according to your promise.

You redeemed your people by your precious blood.
Come, we implore you, to our aid.

    Grant us with the saints
    a place in eternal glory.

Lord, save your people
and bless your inheritance.

Rule them and uphold them
for ever and ever.

Day by day we praise you:
we acclaim you now and to all eternity.

In your goodness, Lord, keep us free from sin.
Have mercy on us, Lord, have mercy.

May your mercy always be with us, Lord,
for we have hoped in you.

In you, Lord, we put our trust:
we shall not be put to shame.

CONCLUDING PRAYER
On this day, Lord God,
you opened for us the way to eternal life
through your only Son's victory over death.
Grant that as we celebrate the feast of his resurrection
we may be renewed by your Holy Spirit
and rise again in the light of life.
(We make our prayer) through our Lord.

www.ingramcontent.com/pod-product-compliance
Ingram Content Group UK Ltd.
Pitfield, Milton Keynes, MK11 3LW, UK
UKHW022244180325
456436UK00001B/5